When They
Crucified
My Lord

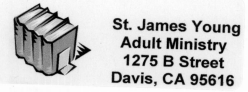
When They Crucified My Lord

Through Lenten Sorrow to Easter Joy

Brother Ramon, S.S.F.

Liguori
LIGUORI, MISSOURI

For Pauline Hillier and Tim Fawcett
who through their Lent entered into Glory
Rest In Peace

Published by Liguori Publications
Liguori, Missouri
http://www.liguori.org

Library of Congress Cataloging-in-Publication Data

Ramon, S.S.F., Brother.
    When they crucified my Lord : through Lenten sorrow to Easter joy / Brother Ramon.—1st U.S. ed.
        p. cm.
    ISBN 0-7648-0710-2 (pbk.)
    1. Lent—Prayer-books and devotions—English. 2. Catholic Church—Prayer-books and devotions—English. I. Title.

BX2170.L4 R36 2001
242'.34—dc21   00–045635

Printed in the United States of America
First U.S. Edition 2001
05 04 03 02 01   5 4 3 2 1

—✠—

Were you there?

Were you there when they crucified my Lord?
Were you there when they crucified my Lord?
Oh, sometimes it causes me to tremble,
    tremble, tremble;
Were you there when they crucified my Lord?
Were you there when they nailed him to the tree?
Were you there when they nailed him to the tree?
Were you there when they pierced him in the side?
Were you there when they pierced him in the side?
Were you there when the sun refused to shine?
Were you there when the sun refused to shine?
Were you there when they laid him in the tomb?
Were you there when they laid him in the tomb?
Were you there when he rose up from the tomb?
Were you there when he rose up from the tomb?
Oh, sometimes it causes me to tremble,
    tremble, tremble;
Were you there when he rose up from the tomb?

FOLK SPIRITUAL

Contents

Introduction

M any inspiring folk spirituals have come down to us as part of
the heritage of Black Americans from the time of slavery, and
these songs can evoke a trembling response when sung by massed
voices. One of the simplest and most direct is "Were you there when
they crucified my Lord?" The question and its response set the tone
of our Lenten book, because constantly the question will arise: "Were
you there?" And if you enter with me right into the center of the drama,
feeling the mystery and responsibility for it all, you will have to respond in the words of the same spiritual: "Sometimes it causes me to
tremble, tremble, tremble...."

We shall be meeting various personalities of the passion in our
Lenten journey—some of them enemies of Jesus, and some whose
hearts were touched with his loving compassion and who were fired
by his call. We shall be able to identify with many, if not all, of them,
and we shall constantly realize our need for a daily conversion and a
new experience of God's grace.

At the end of Lent we come to Easter, and at the end of our Lenten
journey we shall find ourselves outside the garden tomb, trembling
not with fear, nor only with godly awe, but also with hope and joy.

Using This Book

There is a discipline involved. It asks for up to an hour each day of
Lent and, if used with a group, seven weekly meetings. You should set
aside a period at the same time every day and make it sacrosanct, for
it is your meeting-time with God.

If you can, make a worship space for God in some corner or room,
consisting of a low table or shelf, with a candle, an open Bible, perhaps an icon or cross, and some flowers, with a cushion or prayer
stool.

Spend a few minutes centering yourself in the presence and love of God, repeating a Bible or hymn verse, such as, "Breathe on me, breath of God…." Then, when you feel relaxed, take up the day's Scripture, going through it slowly and prayerfully, using different translations which can aid understanding. Follow that with the day's meditation, leading into the prayer, and reflection. Then spend the rest of the time, up to an hour if possible, in prayer and openness before God. End the session with the prayer "Glory be to the Father, and to the Son, and to the Holy Spirit: as it was in the beginning, is now, and ever shall be, world without end. Amen," and carry the theme into your day's work.

Sharing in a Group

Groups may meet on seven occasions, and there is appropriate material in the Appendix. This material may be used freely, but it simply offers suggestions and is not meant to inhibit spontaneity. Groups are at their best between seven and twelve in number, and a wise group leader will encourage all to take part and not let anyone monopolize the rest.

The simplest, humblest experience shared is often the one used by the Lord to benefit others most, and remember that the theme is "trembling," so don't be too nervous to speak. If there is a prepared presentation by a group member, make sure it is not too long and does not inhibit either open discussion or spontaneous contributions.

As you take up this Lenten pilgrimage on a personal or group level, let it enrich your wider experience in the church fellowship. This is a book for any Christian believer who desires to deepen joyful discipleship, and this lesser pilgrimage will minister to your greater journey of faith.

So let's begin.

BROTHER RAMON S.S.F.

Beginning

—✠—

Church and State

ASH WEDNESDAY

Caiaphas: Religious Duplicity

Those who had arrested Jesus took him to Caiaphas the high priest, in whose house the scribes and the elders had gathered....Now the chief priests and the whole council were looking for false testimony against Jesus so that they might put him to death, but they found none, though many false witnesses came forward....The high priest stood up and said, "Have you no answer?..." But Jesus was silent. Then the high priest said to him, "I put you under oath before the living God, tell us if you are the Messiah, the Son of God." Jesus said to him, "You have said so. But I tell you, 'From now on you will see the Son of Man seated at the right hand of Power and coming on the clouds of heaven.'" Then the high priest tore his clothes and said, "He has blasphemed! Why do we still need witnesses? You have now heard his blasphemy. What is your verdict?" They answered, "He deserves death."

MATTHEW 26:57–66

It is a strange thing, but we begin our observation of Lent with the abomination of religion. When religion turns bad it carries with it the stench of corruption, and there is nothing that alienates a person or a people from God like pseudo-religion and hypocrisy (see Isa 1:11–17). And here we are right in the middle of it. The religious authorities, the church of the day, will overturn every rule of justice, every movement of pity, and every claim of truth to hound one man to his death—and that because they cannot bear the fiery gaze of truth and love.

Lest we seem to be exaggerating, let us look at what was happening here. Jesus was arrested in Gethsemane and brought to the house of the high priest, Caiaphas. Matthew sees this as an official meeting of the Sanhedrin (verse 59), composed of Pharisees, Sadducees, and elders, and presided over by the high priest.

Now notice, in this case, the violation of the laws that safeguard justice. First, criminal cases could not be tried during the Passover. If the verdict was "Guilty," a night must elapse before the pronounce-ment was made, so that a recourse to mercy might be made possible. Criminal cases must be tried in the daytime; the meeting should be held in the Sanhedrin Hall of Hewn Stone in the temple precincts; all evidence had to be validated by two witnesses separately examined, and false witness punished by death. On top of all this, evidence for innocence should be presented before evidence for guilt. All these rules were violated. In the midst of witnesses disagreeing, false charges being laid, and for the sake of religious expediency (Jn 11:49–50), Caiaphas pressed both Church and state for the execution of Jesus. And he succeeded.

But here we come to a very strange thing. Behind and through all the malice, hatred, and power struggles, Jesus is seen to be mostly silent, save when the word is needed that will condemn him utterly (verse 64). It is as though *he* is the one who is in control, and that out of the darkest actions of the human heart he can bring good—but only through redemptive suffering.

The Gospel of John sees it clearly, and John's comment may be written over the whole ghastly episode before us. He calls to mind words spoken by Caiaphas to the members of the Sanhedrin when Jesus was engaged in the work of healing, and he was moved to inte-rior jealousy and malice: "You know nothing at all! You do not under-stand that it is better for you to have one man die for the people than to have the whole nation destroyed." And the evangelist shows that even the dark deeds of the human heart at their worst can be turned to ultimate mercy and redemption when he adds: "He did not say this on his own, but being high priest that year he prophesied that Jesus was about to die for the nation, and not for the nation only, but to gather into one the dispersed children of God. So from that day on they planned to put him to death" (Jn 11:49–52).

John is not saying that Caiaphas is predestined to do evil, but that God will bring good out of evil, and will even use the duplicity of evil men to serve the ultimate good. We shall see this again in the case of Judas Iscariot.

Caiaphas was a Sadducee—wealthy, aristocratic, and collaborationist. Sadducees collaborated with Rome as the occupying power, in exchange for money, comfort, and power—and all the priests were Sadducees. Caiaphas, in John's Gospel, is acting in character. He speaks with contempt and arrogance, and his domineering attitude is in contrast to the behavior of Jesus, both here and before Pilate.

The great fear of the Sadducees was that if Jesus gained a following, they would be overthrown, and in the civil disturbance Rome would act against them. They could not think of revolution in terms of love, but only of power—and power is what they had, and wanted to retain. Therefore, they had to appease the greater power and authority of the occupying forces—Rome.

There is a peculiar irony here. Jesus was a revolutionary—not a political and violent messiah (like Judas Maccabeus had appeared to be two centuries previously), but a Messiah of mercy, whose power was the power of love. They thought that if Jesus could be eliminated, the threat would disappear. What they did not know was that because they were eventually successful, judgment fell from a greater authority. In A.D. 70 the Roman military might razed Jerusalem to the ground, and a plow was drawn across the ruined stones of the temple. John's Gospel was written afterwards, and he could perceive the irony of the situation. Yet out of that very situation John could see that not only would Israel be saved, but the Gospel would be proclaimed to the whole world, and the scattered children of God would be brought home to the heavenly Father who longed for their redemption.

When Caiaphas asked Jesus the leading question, "Tell us if you are the Messiah, the Son of God," Jesus need only have made a simple denial, or even kept his silence. But an affirmation was the one thing which would set in motion the whole movement which would make the cross inevitable. Jesus made that affirmation, and so the process was begun.

The church collaborated with the state, as we shall see tomorrow, and the frenzy of venom, hostility, and hatred which is recorded in verses 65–68 began Jesus' *via dolorosa*, the way of sorrows, which took him to the cross.

Prayer

Jesus, condemned and abused: help me to realize how the abuse of religion can lead to hatred, malice, division, and bloodshed—and let me learn more of the religion of redemptive compassion and love. When Church and state stand together against the Messiah of love, help me to take my stand—wherever it may lead.

Reflection

It is not inevitable that Church and state should be corrupted and abused, but they often are. Examine your religion and your political stance at a personal and corporate level, and let God's love purify both, in your thinking and your acting.

— ✠ —

THURSDAY AFTER ASH WEDNESDAY

Pilate: Compromising Politician

Now Jesus stood before [Pilate]; and the governor asked him, "Are you the King of the Jews?" Jesus said, "You say so." But when he was accused by the chief priests and elders, he did not answer. Then Pilate said to him, "Do you not hear how many accusations they make against you?" But he gave him no answer, not even to a single charge, so that the governor was greatly amazed....So when Pilate saw that he could do nothing, but rather that a riot was beginning, he took some water and washed his hands before the crowd, saying, "I am innocent of this man's blood; see to it yourselves." ...So he released Barabbas for them; and after flogging Jesus, he handed him over to be crucified.

MATTHEW 27:11–26

Something very strange is going on here. Jesus is seemingly being judged by Pilate, but as the scene unfolds it emerges that Pilate is being judged by Jesus. By his silence. By his simple innocence and regal attitude.

Poor Pilate is caught up in the web of political and religious machinations, pulled in different directions. He was persuaded of Jesus' innocence, for it was clear that here was no violent revolutionary, yet he was paralyzed in the face of a fanatical religious mob and the state machine. At the end of the narrative, we find him crying out, "What should I do with Jesus?" But it is not simply a question for Pilate, where the roles were reversed in the judgment hall, but also for you and me. "Were you there?" is the question which will continually be asked of us, and the answer is "Yes, I was there." Indeed, it is not a historical question, but a present, existential question which demands an answer today. I remember realizing this as a boy, through the words of an old gospel hymn:

Jesus is standing in Pilate's hall,
Friendless, forsaken, betrayed by all;
Listen! What means now this sudden call:
"What will I do with Jesus?"

"What will I do with Jesus?"
Neutral I cannot be;
Someday my heart will be asking,
"What will he do with me?"

It was not as if Pilate had no guidance. Not only did he have the Christ before him, clothed in innocent simplicity and regal authority, but there was the clear counsel of his wife (Mt 27:19), communicated in a warning dream, to refrain from judgment. And if that was not enough, it was certain that his own heart and conscience revealed the truth. But his will was weak and his courage insufficient for the task.

We are used to the lies and hypocrisies of certain politicians, and Lord Acton's words are enacted in political power structures throughout the world: "Authority everywhere corrupts itself. All power corrupts itself, absolute power corrupts absolutely."

It took but a simple act of courage, an immediate leap of faith, to be true to himself, and to say: "He is innocent; I will not condemn him." But he counted the cost, and decided to compromise, to vacillate, to "hand him over," and in sad guilt and sorrow he washed his hands and tried to put the responsibility on the crowd who seemed willing to assume it.

How easy it is for us, looking back, to condemn Pilate, to blame the authorities, or to participate in the anti-Semitism which makes the Jewish people responsible for the death of Jesus.

"Were you there?" The answer is "Yes." So what will you do with Jesus?

Prayer

Jesus before Pilate: As Pilate stood before you, willing to vacillate, compromise, and hand you over to be crucified, so I see my own attitude reflected at times of weakness and cowardice. Enable me to say: "This will I do with you, Jesus—I will hand my whole self over to you, and own you Lord of all."

Reflection

Consider and reflect on the attitude described by David Kossoff in The Book of Witnesses:

> Once, when I was small, about eight, I was with my father, who was a loving man, in a narrow street in the East End. A huge laborer suddenly roared down at us that we had killed Jesus. My father asked him why he was so unhappy, and the fist lowered and the shouting stopped and he began to cry. We took him with us to my aunt for tea.

FRIDAY AFTER ASH WEDNESDAY

The Crowd: Hosanna and Crucify

The disciples…brought the donkey and the colt, and put their cloaks on them, and he sat on them. A very large crowd spread their cloaks on the road, and others cut branches from the trees and spread them on the road. The crowds that went ahead of him and that followed were shouting, "Hosanna to the Son of David! Blessed is the one who comes in the name of the Lord! Hosanna in the highest heaven!"…

Now the chief priests and the elders persuaded the crowds to ask for Barabbas and to have Jesus killed. The governor again said to them, "Which of the two do you want me to release for you?" And they said, "Barabbas." Pilate said to them, "Then what should I do with Jesus who is called the Messiah?" All of them said, "Let him be crucified!" Then he asked, "Why, what evil has he done?" But they shouted all the more, "Let him be crucified!"

MATTHEW 21:6–9; 27:20–24

A fickle crowd. From "Hosanna" to "Crucify." And all in a few days. We could say that the first crowd broke out in spontaneous affirmation, in celebratory recognition that here he was at last—the one who would fulfill their deepest dreams, their highest hopes—and that the second crowd was manipulated by the scheming politico-religionists who are always biding their time, willing to swing popular opinion and corrupt both religion and politics for their own ends. But that would be a copout.

What we should really see in these two narratives is the split that seems to run right through the human psyche, and through every human person, reflecting both the glory and the shame of our human quest.

We have our dreams—some of them are glorious and some of are nightmares. Both are operative in our personal and corporate lives. We dream them, we put them in motion by dreaming, and we bring them into being for the good and evil of our own souls. Let us look at the two crowds.

The first crowd cried, "Hosanna!" This was a ritual shout, made to a king or a god by an oppressed people, and it meant "Save now." It may be that by Jesus' time it had simply become a shout of welcome and acclamation, but the messianic strands in this narrative remind us of the original meaning. Certainly, the people were oppressed under the Roman heel, and by their own selfish rulers, and the dream of "Messiah" was embedded deep in the national and personal psyche.

One of Jesus' most difficult tasks was to retain the word *messiah*, for he needed to cleanse and redeem it from its violent connotations. The messianic king of the Maccabean dream was a conquering hero, riding into Jerusalem to overthrow the Roman oppressor and cast off its yoke. Jesus retained the word, but purified its meaning. Kings rode both on horses and asses, and the difference was that the horse was a beast of war, but the ass a beast of peace.

Jesus was making the messianic claim (Zech 9:9), but the claim was not to the national throne but to the dedicated hearts of the people. Jesus did not respond to the nationalistic echoes of the cry "Hosanna," but he did come as Messiah. His method of salvation was suffering love, and this begins to unfold in the cry of the second crowd—and many of them would have been the same people.

Certainly, the people were swayed and manipulated. There were crooks planted in the crowd, to ferment mob fanaticism and stir up trouble, so that Pilate would become afraid. Poor Pilate was looking for a way out and offered Barabbas as a face-saving loophole for the people and for himself.

Some ancient Syriac and Armenian versions of our text call him Jesus Barabbas, and both Origen and Jerome knew those readings. Pilate himself twice refers to "Jesus who is called the Messiah" (verses 17, 22), perhaps to distinguish him from Jesus called Barabbas—for it was a common name.

Here then is the offer, with a decision to be made: "Jesus called Messiah, or Jesus called Barabbas?" You would think that the crowd which had welcomed and acclaimed Jesus a few days previously would now confirm and celebrate such affirmation, and welcome Jesus as the Prince of Peace. But the tide seemed to have turned. Before them is a man bound and weakened by ill treatment throughout the night, and around them is a ferment of violence, gesticulation, and threatening behavior, leading the cry, "Barabbas! Barabbas!"

Pilate tried once more, desperately this time, with an appeal to Jesus' innocence. But their blood was up, the mob was in control, the herd mentality had taken over, and even the ordinary, rational people were swept along in the surge of primitive blood lust, "Let him be crucified!"

How easy it seems to take a crowd captive. From the armchair of our comparative democracy in the West, we can look at the television pictures of Eastern Europe and further afield to Third World countries and other cultures and traditions and sit in judgment upon the persecuting blood lust of ethnic cleansing, corrupted elections, military regimes, and wars across diverse tribes and nations where people are manipulated by the power hungry few.

But this narrative is for us, here and now, and the injustices and inequalities are on our own doorstep, within our own politicians and religious leaders of all parties and denominations. And in our own hearts—yours and mine.

Prayer

Jesus, presented to the crowd: Enable me to look into my own heart, my own family, my own nation and continent. Lord, what duplicity I find, and how often I have allowed myself to be manipulated by the power structures of my own party and religion, or by the devices and desires of my own heart. I look upon you, Lord Jesus, in your undeviating innocence and integrity, with a moral courage and true humanity that is far beyond my strength. Meet with me in grace, anoint me by your Spirit, and empower me for your service.

Reflection

It may take what seems to be immense courage to stand against the crowd, to swim against the stream. But in those things which are right, good, and true we should first of all dedicate ourselves, then join with others of like mind, and so be counted for truth, with a proper humility.

SATURDAY AFTER ASH WEDNESDAY

The Soldiers: Scourging and Mocking

Then the soldiers of the governor took Jesus into the governor's headquarters, and they gathered the whole cohort around him. They stripped him and put a scarlet robe on him, and after twisting some thorns into a crown, they put it on his head. They put a reed in his right hand and knelt before him and mocked him, saying, "Hail, King of the Jews!" They spat on him, and took the reed and struck him on the head. After mocking him, they stripped him of the robe and put his own clothes on him. Then they led him away to crucify him.

MATTHEW 27:27–31

When Pilate handed Jesus over to the soldiers, the terrible routine of crucifixion began. Routine to the soldiers, but grief, agony, blood, and death to the Savior.

The soldiers were doing their duty and, though one of my main objections to military service is this matter of unconditional obedience, yet they were least to blame of all those who participated in the passion and death of Jesus. These soldiers were a detachment of the Italian cohort stationed in Palestine at the time and were conscripts from different parts of the empire. The description we have was of horseplay, for Jesus did not see hatred in their eyes as he did in the eyes of the religionists who had delivered him over.

Nevertheless, here was the awful cruelty which began with scourging. Jesus was bound to a post with his back exposed. The lash was a leather thong studded with pellets of bone and lead, and men often died as a result, or went mad. Few retained consciousness throughout the scourging.

There have always been noble soldiers. It is the generals and politicians who must carry the blame for the cruelties and waste of war. But even those who begin with high motivations of crusade and defense, who have been charmed by martial music and heroic stories, are fed powerful propaganda. The fear and violence of battle stir up elementary passions that lead to the brute cruelties and torture which have followed us through holocaust and gulag, through ethnic cleansing and tribal warfare, into our twenty-first century.

So these soldiers, trained to subjugate Rome's oppressed people and detailed for crucifixion duty, began with a charade to a mock king. Yet again, truth was being enacted as they took a soldier's scarlet cloak, a thorny, spiked crown, and a reed scepter, kneeling before Jesus and crying, "Hail, King of the Jews!" This homage paid to Jesus echoed the soldier's salutation to the emperor, "Ave, Caesar, victor, imperator!"

How Jesus reverses the world's values, laying aside military and political pomp and glory, and ascending the throne of the cross, in order that he might subdue the hearts of his people in love.

Jesus willingly and deliberately went the way of the cross, stood before Caiaphas's hatred, Pilate's vacillations, the crowd's fanaticism and the soldiers's mocking. What he did not encounter was indifference. G. A. Studdart Kennedy was, significantly, an army chaplain, and his experience of war informed his poetry. In his collection *The Unutterable Beauty*, he includes a moving poem, "Indifference":

When Jesus came to Golgotha they hanged him on a tree,
They drove great nails through hands and feet and
*   made a Calvary;*
They crowned him with a crown of thorns,
*   red were his wounds deep,*
For those were crude and cruel days and human flesh
*   was cheap.*

When Jesus came to Birmingham they simply
*   passed him by,*
They never hurt a hair of him, they only let him die;
For men had grown more tender, and they would not
*   give him pain;*
They only just passed down the street, and left him
*   in the rain.*

Still Jesus cried, "Forgive them, for they know not
  what they do,"
And still it rained the wintry rain that drenched him
  through and through;
The crowds went home and left the streets without
  a soul to see,
And Jesus crouched against a wall and cried for Calvary.

Here, during the first days of Lent we have come up hard against all these attitudes: hatred, jealousy, compromise, sadistic cruelty, and a charade of mockery. Can we remain indifferent? Before we reach Holy Week, forty days from now, we shall turn to some of the participants in the life and passion of Jesus, and find ourselves among them. And it is well for us to remember that in the midst of all the grief and pain there was one who has been called "John, the beloved." Tomorrow we shall accompany him.

Prayer

Jesus, scourged and mocked: With the soldiers, I have treated sacred things lightly. I have played around with divine truth, and not taken seriously the sacrifice of Calvary. Help me to take my stand among those who betray, deny, or hate you; give me the courage to affirm your humility and compassion, and an inward joy in loving obedience.

Reflection

In our world you will find yourself among those who are enemies of Jesus or indifferent to his love. Without arrogance or self-righteousness, seek to say a quiet word, give a helping hand to victims, sometimes speak out against injustice or cruelty. Such actions will reap their own rewards of joy.

— ✠ —

Lent 1

—✠—

John, the Beloved

LENT 1: SUNDAY

Called From His Nets

As [Jesus] went from there, he saw two other brothers, James son of
Zebedee and his brother John, in the boat with their father Zebedee,
mending their nets, and he called them. Immediately they left the
boat and their father, and followed him.

MATTHEW 4:21–22

The day began as usual. James and John were sitting in the boat doing the necessary work of repairing their nets on the edge of Lake
Galilee, now silent, now conversing with their father, perhaps feeling
that they would like to break out of such a mundane life, doing what
everyone else seemed to be doing in the fish business. Josephus, the
Jewish historian, says that in his day there were 330 fishing boats on
Galilee—not for local consumption only, but for export, even to Rome.

Youth is the time for idealism, for romantic adventure, for laying
your life on the line for a cause, for a principle, for a mighty leader
who can issue the challenge of widening horizons, and impart meaning and purpose into a life hitherto occupied with immediate family,
small anxieties, and parochial business.

John and his brother may well have heard Jesus preach previously, been alerted to his radical message of kingdom repentance, and
spellbound by his works of compassion and healing. But on this day
came the call—a personal challenge of vocation which was impossible to evade. It had to be answered—yes or no. The words of Jesus
are simple, clear, direct, and almost irresistible: "Follow me."

From childhood I was spellbound by mystery. From about ten or
eleven years of age I would wander around the Gower coast of Wales,
aware of the sight, sound, and smell of the sea, allowing myself to be
carried in my solitude into what then seemed to be the vast immensity
of sea and sky, or sometimes in this context I would spend hours in
introspection, which filled the treasure house of my imagination, so
that I still draw upon it.

But one evening, at a missionary service, all this impersonal mysticism became personal, vital, challenging me to decision. I was only twelve years of age and had sat throughout the service listening to one after another of a small group of men and women in their twenties speaking of their call to Christ, and their response in surrendering their lives to him in missionary service overseas.

There was one young woman who carried in her person, shining from her eyes and in the power and simplicity of her words, that clear call: "Follow me." Christ evidently possessed and spoke through her—and I heard his voice. There was no doubting it, and no dodging it. Indeed I did not want to evade the clarity of such an enthusiastic vision.

I responded that evening, and wept my way to the foot of the cross, finding in Christ not only Savior, friend, and brother, but the clue to that strange mystery which I had been exploring in the natural world throughout my childhood, though this did not unfold until years later.

I have never lost that sense of call and vocation. It has been the center and wonder of my life, and though I have sometimes wandered, compromised it, sought lesser loves along the way, and experienced a certain sorrow and pain, I have never wholly lost sight of it. Perhaps I should say "never lost sight of him," for the person of Christ has been the mainspring of my life and motivation. And so it is today. I feel now that heartwarming emotion, those wonderful tears of recognition and childlike joy, that elevation of life and purpose, which came in the first rush of passionate love for Christ. It is still with me, and I am capable of weeping tears of joy and sorrow before the cross as I say compline in my crude chapel fifty years later.

I say that youth is the time for challenge and call, and John doubtless felt that, as he heard the sound of Jesus' challenge to discipleship. How well I understood it as I recall that day of my own call. How my young heart leapt when I first read the words of John Oxenham (1852–1941), which so encapsulate the call of Christ to John the disciple—and to me:

> *Who follows Christ's insistent call*
> *Must give himself—his life, his all*
> *Without one backward look.*

Who sets his hand upon the plough,
And glances back with anxious brow
His calling has mistook.
Christ claims him wholly for his own,
He must be Christ's—and Christ's alone!

What power in those words. What horizons of vision. What call to adventure, to fullness of life, and to whatever the future holds. Ah, there is the nub. If John had known the sweat and tears and blood which were the cost of discipleship, would he have responded? If I had known the paths of glory and pain that I have experienced over the years, would I have assented? There is no doubt about the answer. The call was irresistible, the power was flowing, the challenge was infectious.

This is Lent. There are dark days ahead, but in the flower of youth, in the first flush of enthusiasm, in the glory of vocation, we can understand the words of today's Scripture, "Immediately they left the boat and their father, and followed him."

Prayer

Jesus of Galilee: Your call is clear, gentle, loving, and insistent. Un-stop my deaf ears, open my blind eyes, anoint my fainting spirit, for I would respond in glad and loving obedience. You alone can sound the call, and I can only respond by your grace. So let it be.

Reflection

Perhaps the aimless dissipation of our energies, the listlessness of our spirits, and the lukewarmness of our hearts is because we do not have a center to our lives. The call of Christ is to enthrone him; to take his yoke is to serve him; and the will of Christ is to love him. If you seek to do these things then you will become centered in yourself, and the center of joy and hope to those around you.

—— ✠ ——

LENT 1: MONDAY

Son of Thunder

When the time was come that he should be received up, [Jesus] steadfastly set his face to go to Jerusalem. And sent messengers before his face: and they went, and entered into a village of the Samaritans, to make ready for him. And they did not receive him, because his face was as though he would go to Jerusalem. And when his disciples James and John saw this, they said, Lord, wilt thou that we command fire to come down from heaven, and consume them, even as Elias did? But he turned and rebuked them, and said, Ye know not what manner of spirit ye are of. For the Son of man is not come to destroy men's lives, but to save them....

So he appointed the twelve...James son of Zebedee and John the brother of James (to whom he gave the name Boanerges, that is, Sons of Thunder).

LUKE 9:51–56 (AV); MARK 3:16–17

Yesterday was full of vocation, joy, enthusiasm, burning zeal and a real liftoff of energy, to begin the path of discipleship. Today's readings indicate that conversion is not sanctification. What I mean is that to begin is not to have trodden the path, and a convert is sometimes the opposite of a saint. To have a convert mentality is frequently to hold fanatical opinions, to despise those who do not share them, and even to be willing to persecute in order that your own views should be imposed on others. All these are found in today's readings, and it sends out a clear warning to all converts, religionists, fanatics, and those who think they have a hotline to God or a monopoly on truth.

It is intriguing to look at the textual basis of today's main reading. I believe in positive biblical criticism, but have always been suspicious of the destructive criticism which cuts up the text of Scripture into diverse sources, origins, editors, and copyists, leaving the results in pieces on the slab of critical analysis. Scripture is not to be treated like that, and it is refreshing that there is a swing of the pendulum in contemporary biblical criticism which has redressed the situation. But having said that, it is important to get behind the textual versions and variations to see what is going on, for we do not have any original New Testament documents, but only families of copies, excellent though they are.

There is no problem with the Markan text—Jesus calls James and John Boanerges, or Sons of Thunder. We are not used to thinking of John the disciple as an irascible or violent man. Indeed, he seems to be the one that Jesus loved, the young disciple who was perceptive and utterly devoted to his Lord, leaning upon his breast at the Last Supper, and, if the tradition of his authorship is correct, the disciple who urges his readers to walk in the way of love. The tradition is also strong which speaks of him being carried into the church assembly at Ephesus when he was old and feeble, lifting up his hands and always saying, "Little children, love one another."

But here we have him called a son of thunder, and biblical scholars think those words reflect the Hebrew word for "agitation, excitement, or raging." This is confirmed by our passage from Luke, but we must read it in the Authorized Version, and it is here that our knowledge of textual versions becomes important. The text of the Authorized Version gives full vent to the anger, bad temper, and exclusivist fanaticism of which James and John were capable. Here are converts lacking in sanctification and holiness.

The Samaritan villagers will not receive Jesus because he is a Jew and because his face is set towards Jerusalem. So James and John return furious, and ask Jesus if he will allow them to call down fire from heaven as Elijah did, to burn them up.

Jesus turns to them in sorrow, rebuking them and showing them that their spirit is alien to the gospel he was preaching, and that his mission was a saving work and a redemptive work.

If you take up almost any other translation than the Authorized Version, you will find that the worst fanatical exclusivism is relegated to the footnotes outside the main text. The reason is that the best manuscripts omit the worst language, and the main text must reflect the best literary witnesses.

There may be a number of reasons for such omissions, but I wonder if a copyist simply omitted those sentiments which were so far from the reconciling gospel of Jesus—for, remember, the text was written after the events of Easter and the disciples were a little more sanctified.

You see the point I am making today. It is not enough to be converted—to start along the road, for that is but the beginning of the journey. Without holiness, love, compassion, no one will see the Lord, and we must take our gospel and ethical stance not from the worst actions and words of the Old Testament, but from the covenant as seen through the prism of Christ the Savior and Reconciler. Otherwise, we shall be able to justify polygamy, lying, holy war, crusades, and persecution or execution of those who dissent from our view or lifestyle.

Prayer

Jesus, Savior and Reconciler: May I be truly converted to you, Lord, and not to a religion of opinions and dogmatic tenets. Let my life reflect your compassion, your mercy, and your outgoing love for all in need and misery. May I influence my group, my church, my family, towards an inclusive embrace of all that is good, true and life-giving in our world.

Reflection

Sometimes we behave as if the truth were our truth, and that the only way to maintain it were to impose it, dogmatize it, and enshrine it in tablets of stone. We should look again at the attitude of Jesus towards the "heretical" Samaritans, towards "publicans and sinners," towards the outcasts of society and those who religionists reject. His embrace is wide enough for them all, and so should ours be.

—— ✚ ——

LENT 1: TUESDAY

Ambition and Power

James and John, the sons of Zebedee, came forward to him and said to him, "Teacher, we want you to do for us whatever we ask of you." And he said to them, "What is it you want me to do for you?" And they said to him, "Grant us to sit, one at your right hand and one at your left, in your glory." But Jesus said to them, "You do not know what you are asking. Are you able to drink the cup that I drink, or be baptized with the baptism that I am baptized with?" They replied, "We are able." Then Jesus said to them, "The cup that I drink you will drink; and with the baptism with which I am baptized, you will be baptized; but to sit at my right hand or at my left is not mine to grant, but it is for those for whom it has been prepared."

MARK 10:35–40

The disciples' attitudes do not exasperate Jesus, but they do grieve him. In spite of the charism of his authority, the plainness of his teaching, and the power of his example, they often seemed so thick in the head and hard in the heart.

Yesterday's passage revealed John a novice in the spiritual life, with all his irate anger spilling over as a mania of exclusivism and condemnation. Today's passage is a further example of how far the disciples were from Jesus' understanding of what the kingdom was, or who the Messiah was. The old Maccabean ideas of violent revolution and the political overthrow of the Roman tyranny were still part of their mind-set.

In the previous chapter (9:33–37), the disciples had been arguing as to who was the greatest among them, and Jesus, with infinite patience, had set down a child in their midst as a living example of true conversion and the Christlike life. Then in this chapter (verses 32–34) he had shared with them, for the third time, the warning that on reaching Jerusalem he would be handed over to the religious authorities and begin the dark road of his passion and death.

One would have thought that they all, but especially John, would have been intelligent enough, sensitive enough, aware enough, to realize the pain and grief that had taken hold of Jesus' heart. But in the midst of such sorrow, James and John come to Jesus with a crude request which had emerged straight from their argument about who was to take first place. Their petition was that they should sit at Jesus' right and left hands as ministers of state in his kingdom of power. What kingdom was this? What role did they assume? What were they expecting? Did they still not understand?

Jesus faced them with a stark reply which mirrored to them their ignorance of how things really were, and which asked them if they could drink his cup of suffering, if they could be immersed in the baptism of his passion. They were bold enough to say that they could— for the context of their thinking was so far from his: Yet as Jesus said, they would drink such a cup and be immersed in such a baptism, though they did not know it then.

Yet before we go on to condemn their insensitivity and join with the other disciples in anger at their request (verse 41), we should look at our own understanding of things and interpret our own attitude. The way the Church has interpreted the Christ throughout history has often been a story of imposition, persecution, inquisition, and crusade. The world has looked on, judged rightly, and withdrawn. And Christ has wept anew.

Perhaps we do not so overtly persecute and plunder in Christ's name, but when the occasion arises, for the sake of establishment values, the "defense of our Christian heritage" and the preservation of our economic lifestyle, we will go to war, bless nuclear submarines, or sell arms and military equipment to oppressive regimes and dictatorships around the world. And at a personal level we are willing to participate in and promote a market economy and acquiesce in political manipulation in which money, power, and ambition have primary place.

This is not the whole story, of course, for within the Church and within contemporary political life there are positive forces and good, sensitive men and women who look for justice, equality, and equity. The witness and persistence of the way of Jesus and compassionate humanity continue into our world of paradox and contradiction.

The disciples could not be converted by external example, even though it shone with the radiance of Jesus as the Son of Man. He needed to enter the deep waters of death and plumb the lowest depths of human need and dereliction before the miracle could be accomplished within them.

Yet he gently and firmly put in place the teaching which confirmed his Sermon on the Mount, so that it would be heard, remembered, and recorded for post-Easter days. He took them aside and spoke the words which conclude today's passage, and these words laid down a pattern of personal and political ethics that would revolutionize our nation and world if put into practice. Such a pattern cannot be adopted by unregenerate people, and Jesus knew that. That is why he showed himself as the prototype of this gospel path, and laid down his life to conquer the hearts of his people in love: "The Son of Man came not to be served but to serve, and to give his life a ransom for many" (Mt 20:28).

Prayer

Jesus, Messiah of mercy and truth: Teach me over again the pattern of your humility. Help me to see more clearly that you can be my teacher and example if first of all you become my Savior and indwelling guest. Spell out in my life the personal and corporate implications of walking in the way of sacrifice and simplicity, and then let me live out the life of the gospel in a needy world, in the fellowship of your Church.

Reflection

Imagine the changes which could take place if the Church followed a gospel pattern of simplicity and compassion within its own borders, and as a witness in national and political life. Persecution might follow, but so would the human values of liberation, justice, and truth. Think it through and live it out.

— ✠ —

LENT 1: WEDNESDAY

Transfiguring Light

Jesus took with him Peter, John and James, and went up on the mountain to pray. And while he was praying, the appearance of his face changed, and his clothes became dazzling white. Suddenly they saw two men, Moses and Elijah, talking to him. They appeared in glory and were speaking of his departure, which he was about to accomplish at Jerusalem. Now Peter and his companions were weighed down with sleep; but since they had stayed awake, they saw his glory and the two men who stood with him. Just as they were leaving him, Peter said to Jesus, "Master, it is good for us to be here; let us make three dwellings, one for you, one for Moses, and one for Elijah"—not knowing what he said. While he was saying this, a cloud came and overshadowed them; and they were terrified as they entered the cloud. Then from the cloud came a voice that said, "This is my Son, my Chosen; listen to him!" When the voice had spoken, Jesus was found alone. And they kept silent and in those days told no one any of the things they had seen.

LUKE 9:28–36

The Transfiguration narrative is one of the most beautiful stories in the whole of sacred literature, recorded in all three Synoptic Gospels. It never ceases to dazzle me with its glory and bathe me in its gentle and pure light. The height of the mountain calls me, the radiance from its glory lures me on, and the enlightenment and warmth is kindled to a fiery heat within my heart. All this is witness to a text inspired by the Holy Spirit and capable of rekindling faith and love in its readers perpetually.

Before I joined the Franciscans, I lived for a year with the Community of the Transfiguration in Roslin, near Edinburgh, Scotland. At that time the community had charge of the Sunday Eucharist in the famous and mysterious Roslin Chapel. I say "mysterious" because I felt some strange influences there—a place where light and darkness seemed in conflict. There were some dark stories about the Battle of

Roslin and the bloodshed which was carried into the church of that time, and down into the crypt.

It was the crypt which was most solemn both in its light and darkness. You became aware of the descent below ground level, and if there was no heat it was both dark and damp. But as you descended, you were faced with a glorious window, the base of which was at ground level, while you further descended into the crypt. It depicted the wonderful light and color of the transfiguration, the effulgent Christ, radiating rays of glory towards the dazed disciples, while underneath were the words: "In Your light shall we see light." I felt a creepy sense of historical darkness in that crypt, but also a theological and spiritual sense of glory.

Our text is like that. It is a place of dazzling glory, but also of impending darkness, for here it is that Jesus sets his face and heart toward the cross. Here it is that law and prophet in the person of Moses and Elijah appear in glory, and speak with him about his exodus, the passion which he was to accomplish at Jerusalem. What did the disciples feel about this—especially John? Dorothy L. Sayers caught the spiritual mood perfectly in her episode of this narrative in *The Man Born to Be King*. It needs no further explanation and serves today as our reflection on the text.

Prayer

Jesus, transfigured in glory: Before your passion, the light of the Holy Spirit saturated your being, and the three disciples were enfolded in its radiance. For you it was a confirmation of the rightness of your path through suffering, to glory. For Peter, James, and John, it was a promise of hope, cherished through the darkness of Holy Week, passion, and death. For us all it is a story of glory, a foretaste of heaven, and a participation in the kingdom of light. So let it shine on me, Lord, and let me reflect its glory.

Reflection

The three disciples are conversing quietly during the night following the incident on the mountain. They whisper together on the rooftop of the house where the other disciples are asleep.

Peter: We're all right here, if we talk quietly… It's rather cold.

James: I have brought our cloaks. Look at the stars….Spread above the earth like a robe of glory.

Peter: But nothing to compare with the glory we saw today on the mountain.

James: No. Tell me, Simon Peter—what did you see? Was it the same for all of us?

Peter: I was tired with the climb….I watched him for a time as he stood and prayed, never speaking, never moving, with his face toward Jerusalem…as though he saw nothing but some strange inward vision that held him entranced….I tried to pray, too, but no thoughts would come…it seemed to go on forever….

John: As though time had stopped.

Peter: I think I lost myself a little…there in the silence….for the next thing I knew was a great terror, as though I was drowning in it—and when I looked at his face, it was not of this earth. It was…it was like…it is a thing I dare not think of.

James: Don't, Peter, we saw it too.

Peter: And his garments went whiter than the light—the way no fuller on earth could whiten them….And those two others with him. They spoke together but I couldn't tell what they said….The glory was upon them both and I knew them for blessed Moses that talked with God in Sinai, and holy Elijah who passed up to heaven in light and fire…and it seemed that what I saw was the reality, and the earth and the sky only a dream…yet I knew all the time that the sun was shining, and I could feel the rough stems of heather between my fingers.

James: I had lost touch with everything—except John's hand in mine.

John: Dear James!—I felt you, but as though we were children again—do you remember?—when the great thunderbolt fell, and I was frightened.

John: I was afraid too. Peter was the bravest. He spoke.

Peter: Yes—but such nonsense! I thought the vision was departing. I remember calling out: "Lord—it is good to be here. Can't we build three tabernacles for you and Moses and Elijah, and stay like this for ever?"—so stupid—but I didn't know what I was saying.…

I thought of the Ark in the wilderness and the glory of the Lord in the pillar of fire…all mixed up somehow with the Holy City and the feast of the Tabernacles.…

And then, and then—the fire and the light were all about us…and the Voice…was it without us or within? …and was it a voice at all?

John: It filled everything—there was nothing in the world but the voice: "This is My beloved Son, hear Him."

James: And after that—nothing. Only the hills and the sky, and Jesus standing there alone.

Peter: He held out his hand, and I was afraid to touch him.…But he was just the same…as though nothing had changed him.

John: I think the change was not in him but in us. I think we had seen him for a moment as he always is.…Perhaps the end of the world is quite near.

LENT 1: THURSDAY

Beloved Disciple

Jesus was troubled in spirit, and declared, "Very truly, I tell you, one of you will betray me." The disciples looked at one another, uncertain of whom he was speaking. One of his disciples—the one whom Jesus loved—was reclining next to him; Simon Peter therefore motioned to him to ask Jesus of whom he was speaking. So while reclining next to Jesus, he asked him, "Lord, who is it?" Jesus answered, "It is the one to whom I give this piece of bread when I have dipped it in the dish."

JOHN 13:21–26

L et me say straight away that I believe the beloved disciple to be John. The Johannine texts never explicitly say so, but it is in these texts that he is called "the disciple whom Jesus loved," and these texts so beautifully reflect the devotional and mystical feel of the Johannine context that they present a disciple who already participates in the glory that was to follow at Easter, and with the coming of the Holy Spirit. A close study of today's passage brings us to the edge of this strange mystery.

First of all, we have the picture of Jesus reclining with his disciples at the Last Supper, with the beloved disciples reclining close to his heart. The text actually says *en to kolpo tou Iesou*, in the bosom of Jesus (verse 23). The word *kolpos*, breast or bosom, is the very word used of Jesus dwelling in the intimate heart of the Father, "in the bosom of the Father" (Jn 1:18). The relation of the disciple John to his Savior is likened to that of the Son to the Father. This is mystical indwelling which is at the heart of spirituality as presented in John's Gospel, in which the believer dwells within the bosom of the Son, and the Son dwells within the bosom of the believer. This is to be seen within the context of a wider Trinitarian mysticism in which the believer, and the Church, participate in the very life of the Trinity, and it is already pictured in our passage today.

The upper room is heavy with sorrow as Jesus is troubled in spirit, and he causes a profound stirring of curious grief when he says, "Very truly, I tell you, one of you will betray me." By a simple action (a nod, says the Greek text), Peter indicates to John that he should ask Jesus of whom he was speaking, for all the disciples felt the enshrouding darkness and pain that accompanied the words and spirit of Jesus.

John was the only one who could ask such a question at such a time, and again close attention to the text indicates the intimacy of the moment, for it says, literally, "falling back on the breast of Jesus, he says to him, "Lord, who is it?" John is able to enter into that secret place, to ask the most intimate question, to share the profoundest grief, and to receive the most secret word of Jesus.

This whole process of "falling back" into the secret place indicates that what Jesus says is not for public hearing, not for the world, not even for the other disciples, but for John alone.

A monk friend once told me that he went on pilgrimage to Patmos, and while there visited an old Orthodox *staretz* (hermit). Very little was said as they sat together, but just before the monk left, the *staretz* leaned towards him and said some words which sent him on his way with deep wonder and joy, "John the disciple leaned on the breast of Jesus, and felt the very heartbeat of God."

Prayer

Jesus, man of grief and sorrow: Draw me closer to your heart of love; come and dwell deep within me; grant that in such mystical fellowship and embrace I may manifest the virtues of your grief and joy.

Reflection

It is at the table and altar of the Eucharist that the disciples of Jesus encircle his grief and loving devotion. Ensure that you are present regularly in that place, that you receive the body and blood of his sacrifice, and that by mutual indwelling the world may observe that you have been with Jesus.

LENT 1: FRIDAY

Receiving Jesus' Mother

Standing near the cross of Jesus were his mother, and his mother's sister, Mary the wife of Clopas, and Mary Magdalene. When Jesus saw his mother and the disciple whom he loved standing beside her, he said to his mother, "Woman, here is your son." Then he said to the disciple, "Here is your mother." And from that hour the disciple took her into his own home.

JOHN 19:25–27

This is a simple, but beautiful piece of Scripture. We shall be looking at it again through the eyes of Mary later on in Lent, and through the eyes of Jesus during Holy Week. But today we stand in John's place, as the beloved disciple, faithful to the end.

The monastery where I write is named Saint Mary at the Cross, so this is an appropriate place to be writing today. When I was appointed as superior here, one of the elderly friars, Brother Lawrence Christopher, had become very ill, and it was clear that he was not going to recover. He had been in bed for some days, very frail and weak, and on the day before he died, he asked me if I would let him remain here and not send him away to the hospital. I told him that as we had looked after Brother John some months previously, we would look after him, and that put his mind at rest, and I spoke to him gently and sensitively about how he was feeling in body and spirit.

The next day I was amazed to find him, with his habit on, at our midday office of prayer. He hardly made it, and I had to almost carry him back to bed. When we got there, I helped him off with his habit— I think he had his pajamas on underneath—and his breathing was labored. I said to him, "Lawrence, I'll stay here with you, but I think it would help if you could relax, let go of your tensions and anxieties, and your breathing will become easier." Reassured, as I held his hand, he did just that, and by the time the doctor had arrived he was lying quietly and at rest. He spoke a few sentences to us both, and then went into a sleep in which he slipped into unconsciousness, and the doctor said he would stay a while to see how things went.

Within the hour it became clear that the end was in sight. "I think he is going..." said the doctor. So I knelt by Lawrence's bed, and took his hand, and said the *Nunc Dimittis*: "Lord, now let your servant depart in peace..."

As I came to the end, Lawrence breathed his last. The doctor was moved at the manner of his death, and turning to me, said, "I think he knew he was going." I agreed, and told him of our conversation of the day before.

When the doctor left, I got one of the other friars, Brother Amos, and we placed a sanctuary candle on the cell table, said the prayers for the departing soul, and commended Lawrence to the love of God. Amos went to bed, and I laid Lawrence out, with a deep sense of reverence and peace.

I've related that story under today's Scripture because it is an application of the principle of "companying with the dying," and of the precious privilege it is, simply to be there at such a time. I have been with many people in their dying, due to my medical background, but this one was especially precious because there had been a previous understanding and a genuine trust. Lawrence had been anxious and distressed, and all his fears had been put to rest, and in the event he went gently, but surely, into the nearer presence of his Lord, accompanied by love, prayer, and sacrament. What John the disciple did for Jesus and for Jesus' mother, I did for Lawrence, and it was here, at the monastery of Saint Mary at the Cross.

Today, perhaps you should use this time to consider your relationship to your mother and father, or to older friends who may be depending on you. Or perhaps it is you who are dependent, and you need to allow your children or loved ones to care for you, and to let go of some of your stubborn independence.

Our Lord lost all his independence when his hands and feet were nailed to the cross. He could not stretch out his arms in physical support of his grief-laden mother, or take her back home that evening in her sorrow and grief. But John could. And did.

Whether your task today is to give an open heart and a helping hand to someone who needs you, or to allow them to care for you—here at the cross is the place of forgiveness, absolute trust, and simple surrender.

John's eyes were full of tears, but he was not blinded by them; his arms felt heavy, but he supported Mary in her need; his legs were trembling, but when he heard the dying words of Jesus, "Here is your mother," he folded her to himself in love. And there is a world of meaning in the final words, "And from that hour the disciple took her into his own home."

Prayer

Jesus, dying Savior: Even in the hour of your death, your loving tenderness did not fail. You held Mary and John in your heart even when your hands were crucified. Grant that I may be faithful to those you have committed to my care, both in their living and their dying. And grant that when my time comes, I may have a good and gentle death, loved on earth and received, by your grace, in heaven.

Reflection

Think today on your own situation. Has God called you to care for a loved one, either spiritually or physically? Are you faithful to your task? Are you being cared for at any level by another—in body or spirit? Are you showing openness and gratitude, and letting go of any selfish or stubborn independence born not of thoughtfulness, but of pride? Let go of such attitudes, and any anxieties or fears, and let God breathe his peace into your troubled spirit.

LENT 1: SATURDAY

John, the Gospel Witness

Jesus did many other signs in the presence of his disciples, which are not written in this book. But these are written so that you may come to believe that Jesus is the Messiah, the Son of God, and that through believing you may have life in his name....

There are also many other things that Jesus did; if every one of them were written down, I suppose that the world itself could not contain the books that would be written.

JOHN 20:30–31; 21:25

The Gospel of John is one of the most profoundly spiritual and mystical books in the world. If you want to do some scholarly research on it, look at the excellent commentary by Raymond E. Brown (*The Gospel According to John*, Doubleday, 1969). But this is not the place for critical study—we are rather concerned with the Gospel which bears John's name.

During this week of Lent, it has become clear that a mighty work of conversion and sanctification has been taking place in John the disciple, from his early call from his nets at the Lake of Galilee, through an exclusivism and dogmatism that had no place in the kingdom of Jesus, then ascending the mountain where he, as well as Jesus, became transfigured in his personality, and the descending into the dark path which led to the foot of the cross. In the process he was transformed, and the whole Gospel of John as we now have it, is the reflection upon such experiences, translated into the all-embracing gospel of the universal Christ.

We have a long and difficult Lenten path to tread, but today's Scripture shines with hope and promise upon the thorny road. It is a foretaste of the fact that light will overcome darkness, and that ultimately love cannot be defeated by crucifixion, but will rise in newness of life for those who have followed all the way.

Since Ash Wednesday we have had to confront the worst that evil can do in the face of the divine love. Jesus is taken by the wicked hands of Church and state, and betrayed to death after torture and suffering. But the New Testament documents which tell us the dark story are part of the good news. And the good news is that the light shines in the darkness, and the darkness will never be able to extinguish it (Jn 1:5). The Gospel of John is really a gospel tract. It is written not as a piece of historical research, or as a coldly objective narrative or biography, but as a document of salvation—God's love-letter to a dark world, to tell them that the light continues to shine, and that we all may be illumined and warmed by its radiance.

Overfamiliarity with this Gospel can dull our appreciation of its radical story, and if we simply ask for opened eyes and renewed hearts we shall be able to enter into the joy and tears, the excitement, adventure and discovery of life, light and love that pulsate in its pages.

The verses at the beginning of today's study are a kind of vantage point from which the Gospel is to be viewed, and make clear the purpose of its writing—actually to communicate in living experience the very life of Jesus which lights up the stories and narrative. Originally the Gospel finished at the end of chapter twenty, where this wonderful declaration of intent appears. But in chapter twenty-one we have some additional material which the writer wanted to include because of the sheer Resurrection joy which it contains. Then at the very end (21:25), the writer is almost bursting with joy as he tells us that the whole world is too small for the wonderful stories of life and love that could be told. But here, in this Gospel of John, there is enough to set our hearts aflame.

Prayer

Jesus, Savior of the world: Help me to approach the Gospel of John with a cleansed heart, an open mind, and anointed eyes. Let me see again the way in which Jesus lived and loved in our dark world, shedding his light, radiance, and healing forgiveness along the way. And then incarnate such love in me, that I may shine in my dark corner with increasing radiance.

Reflection

Let today's study affirm the rightness of the time you are setting aside for this work of prayer and reflection during Lent. And be determined, after Easter, to take up the Gospel of John again, with prayerful dedication, and let it accomplish in you what God intends—to his praise and your joy.

—— ✠ ——

Lent 2

—✠—

Peter, the Rock

LENT 2: SUNDAY

Follow Me

As [Jesus] walked by the Sea of Galilee, he saw two brothers, Simon, who is called Peter, and Andrew his brother, casting a net into the sea—for they were fishermen. And he said to them, "Follow me, and I will make you fish for people." Immediately they left their nets and followed him.

MATTHEW 4:18–20

Jesus' call "Follow me" to Peter was different from that made to John. It was not so much that the words or the context changed, but the inward attitude to which he spoke was a whole different world. John was a young man with all the sense of zeal, adventure, lure, and romanticism which was summoned up with the call of Jesus. When it came, it lit the touch point of John's soul, and he left his nets, his father, the prosperous business, and cast himself unreservedly with all the joy of youth, at Jesus' feet. He could have said:

Just as I am, young, strong and free,
To be the best that I can be,
For truth, and righteousness, and Thee,
Lord of my life—I come.

But Peter was different. He was not "in the glad morning of his day." He was older, more mature, with wife, mother-in-law, responsibilities, poorer than John and more of a common, working man. Perhaps he was somewhat world-weary, and he was certainly a bit rash, impetuous, and awkward in his dealings with others. His version of the matter would be:

Just as I am, though tossed about
With many a conflict, many a doubt,
Fightings and fears within, without,
O Lamb of God, I come.

CHARLOTTE ELLIOTT (1789–1871)

When the call of Jesus comes, it meets our individual needs, and it is not simply a matter of his words, but the manner in which they are spoken, the nuance of his appeal, the subliminal communication which runs along the hidden network of our emotional and spiritual needs—until we are caught—like fish in a net. For it was Christ the master fisherman who was at work that day.

Jesus calls us, and correlates that call to our need. He begins where we are. In Peter's case it is with the matter of nets and fish, up to his waist in the waters of Galilee.

We are caught, not like a con man catching his victim, robbing and shaming them, but like a loving mother or father catching their child, like a player catching a ball, like a trapeze artist catching the flyer, like a lover catching the beloved.

So Jesus, the master fisherman, caught Peter for his salvation. And once caught, Peter realized it was a liberating bondage, a perfect freedom. There were dark days ahead, bold affirmation and shameful denials, but always, always the divine love was there before him, clothing, enfolding, embracing, and surrounding him. So that he, too, became a fisherman who would catch souls for his Lord.

Prayer

Jesus, Master Fisherman: Catch us, Lord, within the net of your salvation, that we may rejoice in the meshes of your love. Then help us to spread the gospel net, that others may be drawn into the kingdom, and become the disciples of the gospel and the bearers of joy.

Reflection

The gospel net is a network of fine, strong cords, woven compassion and joy. Keep your net in good repair, share your net with others, and become master fishermen, with Jesus, in the work of the kingdom.

— ✛ —

LENT 2: MONDAY

Wife and Mother-in-Law

When Jesus entered Peter's house, he saw his mother-in-law lying in bed with a fever; he touched her hand and the fever left her, and she got up and began to serve him. That evening they brought to him many who were possessed with demons; and he cast out the spirits with a word, and cured all who were sick. This was to fulfill what had been spoken through the prophet Isaiah, "He took our infirmities and bore our diseases."

MATTHEW 8:14–17

The Bible gives mothers-in-law a good press. Naomi, in the book of Ruth, was a mother-in-law to be loved and honored in daily life (Ruth 1:1–17). And here, Peter's mother-in-law had a wonderful story to tell of sickness, restoration, and service.

It is a remarkable fact that far from being a celibate, hierarchical figure, the Peter of our reading is not only a family man, but one who carries the gospel right into the heart of his home, for his house was the base that Jesus used when ministering in Capernaum.

And it didn't stop there. For, in later days, when Peter led the band of apostles and went out on missions of evangelism, instruction, and healing, he took his wife with him (1 Cor 9:5). It would be intriguing to know the forms of ministry in which she was involved.

The story of Peter's mother-in-law's healing is set in the context of Jesus' teaching and healing in the synagogue on the Sabbath day (see Mk 1:21–34). Here, his healing power is called forth again, and towards evening Peter's house was surrounded by possessed and sick people in need of his touch.

The ministry was costly, for as we are reminded in Mark 5:30, power went out of Jesus when he healed the sick. Therefore, at the end of the day, he must have been very tired, and Matthew relates this costly ministry to that of the suffering servant of Isaiah 53, when he quotes, "He took our infirmities and bore our diseases."

The early Church took up this suffering servant theme in proclaiming Jesus as Savior, healer and Messiah, and saw the whole ministry of Jesus as a holistic one, so that salvation was not merely of the "soul" but of the whole person. Salvation, in its fullness, means a whole body, a clear mind, and a pure heart. Such fullness is reserved for the life of heaven, but we may have a foretaste of it now, realizing the holistic way in which Jesus gave himself, which is the price of suffering love.

The healing of Peter's mother-in-law is a domestic scene. Jesus was not acting as a magician, nor healing as a persuading wonder-worker before an admiring public, but simply because the woman was sick. She probably had the kind of malaria common around marshy ground where the river Jordan entered and left the lake of Galilee. Mosquitoes abounded there, and the symptoms were jaundice, sweating, shivering, and enervating exhaustion.

The story is told in all the Synoptic Gospels. Matthew says that Jesus touched her, Mark that he took her hand and lifted her, and Luke that he ordered the fever to leave her. In all cases, the response is immediate, glad, and generous—she offered her loving service in waiting upon them.

Prayer

Jesus, whose touch is healing: Stretch out your hand and touch me today. Lift me up from my sins, sickness, and lethargy and order my anxieties and worries to depart. Thus I shall be able to serve you in the house of prayer, and in your suffering people who I meet day by day—imparting to them your healing touch.

Reflection

In your life, how wide are its applications and sympathies of the healing power of Christ.

— ✠ —

LENT 2: TUESDAY

Bold Affirmation

Then Jesus said to them, "You will all become deserters because of me this night; for it is written, 'I will strike the shepherd, and the sheep of the flock will be scattered.' But after I am raised up, I will go ahead of you to Galilee." Peter said to him, "Though all become deserters because of you, I will never desert you." Jesus said to him, "Truly I tell you, this very night, before the cock crows, you will deny me three times." Peter said to him, "Even though I must die with you, I will not deny you." And so said all the disciples.

MATTHEW 26:31–35

This passage needs to be read over carefully and prayerfully two or three times because it is like a mirror, and we are reflected in it, in all our hopes and weaknesses.

It is just because he loved Jesus that Peter blustered and made such an impetuous claim and affirmation. Jesus had held up the mirror of truth into which he gazed deeply. And in response or reaction, he had said something like, "Jesus, Lord, I would never desert you; I would never abandon you. Whatever Matthew and Thomas and James do, I'll not deny you, even if I must die with you—for I love you." All the others affirmed their loyalty, too, but Peter did it boldly because that was the kind of man he was. And he meant it. He truly loved Jesus, and he thought he could stand up in the evil day. But Jesus knew better.

Jesus quoted the book of Zechariah (13:7), into which messianic prophecies were woven, and which he saw fulfilled, as the shadow of the cross enshrouded him and the circle of his disciples.

There is a time to be bold for the Lord, to be counted among those who follow and serve him, and even to take great risks and leaps of faith in loyalty to your Savior. But this can only be done in the power and grace of Christ, and only after you have counted the cost of discipleship.

Jesus himself had warned the disciples about not counting the cost (Lk 14:25–33), and had said specifically, "No one who puts a hand to the plow and looks back is fit for the kingdom of God" (Lk 9:62). But Peter had not heard—or was overconfident.

There would come a time, after his sanctification and maturity, that he would manifest the ultimate loyalty and lay down his life in martyrdom. But between this incident and that witness of glory there was denial, tears, remorse, and weeping—a time of repentance, restoration, and spiritual renewal. The path is long, and none of us are either worthy or strong enough to tread it unaided.

The Gospel is the good news of grace. That means that we are loved and accepted not because we are worthy, loyal, or boldly affirmative, but simply because we are needy sinners. If we realize that, if we confess our sins, then we shall find ourselves "ransomed, healed, restored, forgiven," and empowered by the Holy Spirit. In those circumstances loyalty will be possible because Christ will be our strength.

Let us look into the mirror which Jesus placed before Peter. Let us take the measure of our own weakness, and learn from the example of this well-meaning man who believed too much in his own ability to withstand his own fears.

Prayer

Jesus, smitten Shepherd: Like Peter, I have made blundering claims and bold affirmations, and like him, in the hour of need I have been found wanting. Let me gaze into your mirror of truth, and learn to live in the realities of my own weakness, and thus will I be led to true humility and a deeper dependence on your grace.

Reflection

Think about your friends. Do some of them behave like Peter with his bold claims and confident affirmations, and then fall by the way? Do others of them evaluate their true situation and in humble dependence take each task, each day, each relationship, in gentleness and trust? Begin today to let this lesson do its work in your heart.

LENT 2: WEDNESDAY

Wash Me Thoroughly

Jesus knew that his hour had come to depart from this world and go to the Father. Having loved his own who were in the world, he loved them to the end....And during supper Jesus, knowing that the Father had given all things into his hands, and that he had come from God and was going to God, got up from the table, took off his outer robe, and tied a towel around himself. Then he poured water into a basin and began to wash the disciples' feet and to wipe them with the towel that was tied around him. He came to Simon Peter, who said to him, "Lord, are you going to wash my feet?" Jesus answered, "You do not know now what I am doing, but later you will understand." Peter said to him, "You will never wash my feet." Jesus answered, "Unless I wash you, you have no share with me." Simon Peter said to him, "Lord, not my feet only but also my hands and my head!"

JOHN 13:1–9

When I served at Saint Mary's Episcopal Cathedral, in Glasgow, Scotland, one of my tasks for the Holy Thursday service was to seek out twelve people to participate in the foot-washing ceremony. Some were eager, some were honored, and some were reticent.

Marion was shy, so in her case I said, "Marion, you will find it such a wonderful experience if you will just allow yourself to take part." She did and, afterwards, she said, "I felt so insignificant when the bishop took off his chasuble, bound the towel round his waist, and knelt at my feet, washed and kissed them...but then so precious...."

She had discovered the joy of submission, obedience, and humility. This is what the story is about. It is an enacted parable of the glory of Jesus who laid aside his divine glory, stooped to become one of us, girded himself with our humanity, and knelt at our feet in lowliness and love.

When the disciples arrived at the upper room, there were the towels and water pots, but having had their argument about who was the greatest, none of them would take the menial task of the slave and perform the usual foot-washing. Once you have proudly made your stand, spoken your opposition, countered your opponent, it is then difficult to retrace your steps, take back the hasty word and apologize.

So Jesus, in the atmospheric context of coldness and pride, was the one to bend—on their behalf. You can imagine the growing discomfort and unease as he removed his outer garment, girded himself with a towel, and knelt in the silence, unloosing the thong of the first sandal, taking the foot gently, washing, and passing on to the next disciple. Not a word was spoken until he came to Peter.

Peter felt he was going to explode, and with a rush of mingled penitence and impetuosity he drew his feet away, saying, "Lord, are you going to wash my feet?" Jesus, kneeling, looked up into his eyes, and said, "You do not know now what I am doing, but later you will understand."

What a word this is for the season of Lent, and for our lives, surrounded by the perplexities of what it means to be human. A loved one is suddenly taken in midlife; opportunities long worked for are snatched away and given to another; sickness and anguish invade our own being, and we are burdened at the suffering and pain that pours each day from the TV screen.

Into such perplexity and darkness, Jesus speaks his saving word that even those things which are not sent by God will be taken up into the greater good, and that the spoiled pattern upon the loom of our life will yield to a more profound interpretation in the wider knowledge of the kingdom of God.

Peter would understand in the future. The present task is to submit, to yield, to surrender himself to the loving touch and cleansing which Jesus offers. "Unless I wash you, you have no share with me," replied Jesus. And Peter's impetuous affection spilled over, and the pendulum swung completely in the other direction, "Lord, not my feet only but also my hands and my head."

With all his faults, there was something lovable, warm, and completely human about Peter—and Jesus understood it, and ministered to his deepest need. Once Jesus touched that tender spot in Peter's soul, he yielded, laid aside his stubbornness and independence, and

simply "allowed" Jesus to take his feet caressingly, gently, firmly—
and he began to understand.

There was a lot of darkness ahead, and this was the first of many
lessons in which Peter would stumble, fall, deny, and run away, but it
was a lesson truly learned. Afterwards, he looked back and saw this
experience as a watershed, yielding its meaning in so many aspects of
his future life of ministry, leadership, and suffering—leading to the
ultimate understanding of glory.

Prayer

*Jesus, girded with the towel: You kneel before me when I should fall at
your feet; you embrace me tenderly when loving affection should be
my heart's initiative; you ask me to allow you to minister to my deepest needs. I realize, in part, that so much of my life is lived by faith,
and that I must believe you where I cannot see, and trust you where I
cannot prove. Today, Lord, let me surrender to your tender care, and
then let me gird myself with the towel of service, and do for others
what you have done for me.*

Reflection

*Learn the lesson that you cannot serve unless you are served; that
you cannot love unless you are loved. Yield, surrender yourself to the
loving forgiveness and cleansing that Christ offers, and then let his
spirit of humble service mark your life. Nothing is too menial or insignificant for him, and therefore for you. So look out today for one
simple task—the opportunity he gives you to serve in his name.*

— ✠ —

LENT 2: THURSDAY

The Spirit Is Willing

Then Jesus went with them to a place called Gethsemane; and he said to his disciples, "Sit here while I go over there and pray." He took with him Peter and the two sons of Zebedee, and began to be grieved and agitated. Then he said to them, "I am deeply grieved, even to death; remain here, and stay awake with me." And going a little farther, he threw himself on the ground and prayed, "My Father, if it is possible, let this cup pass from me; yet not what I want but what you want." Then he came to the disciples and found them sleeping; and he said to Peter, "So, could you not stay awake with me one hour? Stay awake and pray that you may not come into the time of trial; the spirit indeed is willing, but the flesh is weak."

MATTHEW 26:36–41

W hen I first began seriously to explore the hermit life in 1990, I left Glasshampton monastery and took off with a modest-sized mobile home to the grounds of Tymawr convent in Wales. As I stood at the entrance to the plum orchard enclosure, it was the beginning of September, and I realized that in the winter ahead, with no heat, I would be experiencing perhaps more asceticism than I had bargained for, and thought that perhaps my health would suffer. But the spirit was willing.

I was not into asceticism, but into answering our Lord's call to love, prayer, and solitude, though I don't believe he was asking me to freeze. My attitude was that of many men or women who start out on an adventure which will take its physical toll. It is not that you weigh the pros and cons, and come to a considered decision. After all, it is an adventure, an exploration, and because the spirit is willing, you go for it.

Well, it happened. During the second winter, with ice inside and outside my dwelling place, one night I had an alarming episode of vertigo and soaring blood pressure. I realize now, in retrospect, that I was probably affected by hypothermia, for even with seven layers of clothing, at 4.30 A.M. during my time of meditation I could still feel the cold seeping through.

I eventually sent to see the local doctor—a warm-hearted Irishman, to whom I said, "You probably think that what I am doing is crazy." "Oh no," he replied, "I don't think it is crazy at all; it is important. But the way you are doing it is crazy." And he made me promise I would get a source of heat if I was to continue. So I did. The spirit was willing, but I did not take sufficient notice of the fact that the flesh was weak.

Yesterday we found that even Peter's objection to Jesus washing his feet had an impetuous affection and contrition about it. He felt he was not worthy and that he should have been on his knees before Jesus. He learned a deep lesson in humility there, but the short time that had passed had taken him into the deep waters of sorrow, grief, and exhaustion.

In Gethsemane, Peter felt the horror and abandonment that was opening up before Jesus, and he glimpsed the burden that was weighing upon the Savior. As a boy, the description of Gethsemane communicated its awful mystery to me. I read it in the old Authorized Version of the Bible then, and it is those words which still reverberate in my heart: "And they came to a place which was named Gethsemane. …And he taketh with him Peter and James and John, and began to be sore amazed, and to be very heavy; And saith unto them: My soul is exceeding sorrowful unto death: tarry ye here, and watch" (Mk 14:32–34 AV).

And Luke adds even more harrowing verses: "And there appeared an angel unto him from heaven, strengthening him. And being in an agony he prayed more earnestly: and his sweat was as it were great drops of blood falling down to the ground" (Lk 22:43–44 AV).

The word *Gethsemane* means "oil press," and it was here that Jesus was being crushed under the grief and burden of the world's sorrow and sin—crushed so that the virgin oil of balm and forgiveness could be poured into the world's gaping wounds.

His spirit was willing, for he had completely surrendered himself to the will of the Father come what may. The weakness of his flesh did not deter him from following to the end of the road, and that meant death on the cross.

Peter *wanted* to share, to enter in, to stand with Jesus in the deep hour of his need, and that is the reason why Jesus brought him, with James and John, to Gethsemane, to be with him, to watch, to be there for him as desolation threatened his very soul.

When Jesus said, "I am deeply grieved, even to death, remain here, and stay awake with me," it looked as if he may have died in Gethsemane—and that was not the way. Peter heard the words, partly understood, and because his spirit was willing he tried to stay awake. He steeled himself against the exhaustion which was the result of his inner turmoil, but he couldn't do it.

We cannot blame Peter here, for we should not have got as far as Gethsemane. Our spirit is willing only when the gospel means something like the joy of forgiveness, physical healing, or self-fulfillment and mental integration. But when we are challenged to deny ourselves, to take up our cross to follow Jesus, when we are told to go out alone into the wilderness, to give our money to the poor and to become the servant of all, then we realize that we are not as willing as we thought. We want a gospel that will enhance our lives, make us popular, likable, successful, and prosperous, and we would fight, and even kill, for our "Christian way of life" because we have come to believe that it is an expression of our Western, capitalist lifestyle of economic growth and material advantage in the marketplace.

Jesus calls us to Gethsemane where our life is utterly yielded to God, so that his will may be done, and to Calvary where our egocentric values are shown up for what they are, and we have to die to self. I am not preaching a gospel of asceticism, but rather of putting our lifestyle and values in the context of an athlete's willingness of spirit to forgo superfluous luxuries and shoddy living for the sake of winning the prize. This is the pattern of Jesus, and it was what he called Peter to follow, spelled out in these words: "Jesus…who for the sake of the joy that was set before him endured the cross, disregarding its shame, and has taken his seat at the right hand of the throne of God" (Heb 12:2).

The amazing thing is that the only way this gospel path can be traveled is if your eyes are upon the coming glory. And the joyful experience is that once your feet are set firmly upon the path with a willing spirit, then that future glory shines backwards into the present, and you have a foretaste of heaven in the shadows of Gethsemane, just as Jesus was strengthened by angelic ministry in his darkest Gethsemane prayer.

Prayer

Jesus of Gethsemane: I thought my spirit was willing, but as I begin to realize the thorns and briars on the way, I am afraid and beset by doubts and conflict. Give me the vision of glory that sustained you, my Lord, in your pilgrimage, and as I identify with the failure and sorrow of Peter in exhausted sleep, renew my will, fortify my desire, and inflame my love.

Reflection

It is not God's will to dampen or dissuade a willing spirit, but rather to strengthen and encourage the fainting heart to greater endeavor. Take heart from this principle, avail yourself of Christ's grace, and encourage those around you who show willingness of spirit to follow the Lord.

LENT 2: FRIDAY

The Flesh Is Weak

They went to a place called Gethsemane; and [Jesus] said to his disciples, "Sit here while I pray." He took with him Peter and James and John, and began to be distressed and agitated. And he said to them, "I am deeply grieved, even to death; remain here, and keep awake." And going a little farther, he threw himself on the ground and prayed that, if it were possible, the hour might pass from him. He said, "Abba, Father, for you all things are possible; remove this cup from me; yet, not what I want, but what you want." He came and found them sleeping; and he said to Peter, "Simon, are you asleep? Could you not keep awake one hour? Keep awake and pray that you may not come into the time of trial; the spirit indeed is willing, but the flesh is weak."

MARK 14:32–42

Today we shall consider the words, "The flesh is weak." This is the story of our human life. So many noble endeavors begin in moments of vision, glimpses of glory, resolutions of dedication, but along the way, because of compromise, difficulty, or temptation, the flesh gives way, and the vision dims into the light of common day, and even into abject failure.

Remember that Peter's earlier bold affirmation not only promised loyalty in life, but obedience unto death. It was a bold claim, and he meant it. He certainly had a willing spirit. But in the event, the powers of darkness and his inner turmoil overcame him, so that he fell into an exhausted sleep out of sheer fear and weariness. The flesh is weak. Again, we must not stand in superior judgment, for we have never been exposed to such terror and darkness as were unleashed in the Garden of Agony.

When I made my second six months' experiment in solitude on the edge of the Lleyn Peninsula in North Wales in the winter of 1983–1984, I had a strange confrontation with darkness that was completely new and which terrified me. It was in the cold darkness of an early

51

February morning, and I had been using material from Amnesty International to pray for prisoners of conscience, tortured and abused. My experience was that I held them before God in prayer and silence, entering into an empathetic understanding of their helplessness, praying that healing, hope, and joy may be infused into their situation. This had been my practice for some years, and it was undergirded by a theology of prayer which still bears positive meaning for me.

But on this occasion, without warning, instead of my injecting hope and healing into their darkness, I was suddenly confronted with a raw darkness and evil, poised to attack me. It was dark, and although I did not physically see color, I had the distinct impression of a red flashing light of warning as the powers of darkness began to move towards me, so I stopped and quickly withdrew from that place where my meditation had taken me.

I was very frightened, for geographically I was alone on the Anelog Mountain, surrounded by icy darkness, with no one within reach or call. In retrospect, I know now that this confrontation with dark powers was allowed by the Lord—though held in check—in order to show me, as my spiritual director Mother Mary Clare, S.L.G., later explained, that I was unprepared to enter such profound intercession and conflict with dark powers.

She assured me that it was part of my way for the future, but that now it was premature, and I must not experiment in such dark places until I was prepared, armed, and called into such a ministry by the grace of the Lord. A salutary word—for the flesh is weak.

My darkness was nothing compared to that which invaded Gethsemane, for if you turn back and read again the quotation from Matthew and Mark concerning the intense burden which descended upon Jesus, you will see that an abyss of desolation and abandonment opened up before him. It was that experience which caused him to fall on his face on the ground in such agony of prayer that brought him to the edge of death, when his sweat was, as it were, great drops of blood falling to the ground.

The words from these quotations are fearful, and modern translations have struggled to find ways of communicating the pain and grief, the fear and terror reflected in the Greek text. We read that Jesus was *sore amazed, very heavy, exceeding sorrowful unto death, in an agony.*

It was as if Peter had stumbled into the private garden where the struggle and conflict between heaven and hell was taking place. The beginning of Jesus' wrestling with dark powers in his passion is found here. It is an awesome place, and even though Jesus chose Peter and his companions to be near him in his hour of utter need, they could not stay awake. They slept not simply through exhaustion, but because of the cold and clammy fear that surrounded them, so that they could not face staying awake and confronting it in Gethsemane.

You can imagine something of the enervating draining of courage and confidence that Peter felt on waking to Jesus' words, "Are you still sleeping and taking your rest? Enough. the hour has come; the Son of Man is betrayed into the hands of sinners" (14:41). There were voices, lanterns, and a garbled exchange and skirmish. All the disciples deserted Jesus and fled into the darkness. Including Peter. The flesh is weak.

Prayer

Jesus alone in the Garden: I have not been exposed to the turmoil and darkness that Peter experienced in Gethsemane, for I have hardly been tested at such a level. My spirit is willing, but my flesh is weak. Therefore, prepare me well before any conflict; gird me with the grace of your Spirit and the armor of God; enable me to understand this dimension of darkness, and keep me faithful in the fight. I believe the victory is with love, and I want to be willing to follow you to the cross.

Reflection

These last two days we have been glimpsing the deeper reaches of prayer, where spiritual battles are fought and won. In your own daily prayers, remember those who are called to such ministries of prayer, and be open to God, with the possibility that you may be called to such a ministry.

LENT 2: SATURDAY

Denial

They took Jesus to the high priest; and all the chief priests, the elders, and the scribes were assembled. Peter had followed him at a distance, right into the courtyard of the high priest; and he was sitting with the guards, warming himself at the fire....While Peter was below in the courtyard, one of the servant-girls of the high priest came by. When she saw Peter warming himself, she stared at him and said, "You also were with Jesus, the man from Nazareth." But he denied it, saying, "I do not know or understand what you are talking about." And he went out into the forecourt. Then the cock crowed. And the servant-girl, on seeing him, began again to say to the bystanders, "This man is one of them." But again he denied it. Then after a little while the bystanders again said to Peter, "Certainly you are one of them; for you are a Galilean." But he began to curse, and he swore an oath, "I do not know this man you are talking about." At that moment the cock crowed for the second time. Then Peter remembered that Jesus had said to him, "Before the cock crows twice, you will deny me three times." And he broke down and wept.

MARK 14:53–54, 66–72

From the words "Peter followed at a distance" to the words, "he broke down and wept," there is a world of harrowing experience, compounded of courage and hope, of sudden fear and momentary cowardice, of grieving love, and a broken heart.

Where did this story come from? Who could have written it so movingly, so honestly, so powerfully? It is one of the most gripping narratives of the Bible, and the fact is that it came from Peter himself. He did not paper over the cracks, make excuses for the downright cowardice and slippery slope of denial.

Papias, the second-century historian, tells us that Mark was Peter's interpreter, and that he wrote down accurately, though not in order, what Christ had said and done from the preaching of Peter.

Far from evoking a spirit of critical condemnation in the reader, this passage draws out of us a deep sympathy for the plight in which Peter found himself. Indeed it was a wonder that he had come so far from the abandonment of all the disciples in Gethsemane, and made his way right into the courtyard of the high priest. It was not bravado, curiosity, or desperation that brought him there, but a loving heart that did not know how to act, which way to go, and was trying to come to terms with the horror of Gethsemane, and the frustrated attempt at violent rescue when he cut off the ear of Malchus, the high priest's servant (Jn 18:10). All the Synoptic Gospels report this incident, but it was too dangerous to name the disciple until John's Gospel was written, decades later.

So the first thing we should understand about this passage is that Peter, though following at a distance, had come so far. How wonderful it would have been if he had bridged even that distance and come right up to Jesus' side, and said, "This man is my Master and Lord, and where he goes, I go."

Then the gospel writer would have reported, "The soldiers, their officer, and the Jewish police arrested Jesus, and his disciple Peter, and bound them. They took them to Annas, who was the father-in-law of Caiaphas, the high priest..." (cf. Jn 18:12–13). The story would have turned out so differently for Peter.

The course of the redeeming work of Christ would have continued—though Jesus would have looked upon Peter with grateful compassion, and Peter would have still gone to his martyrdom—though a few years earlier. But that was not to be. And perhaps, for our sakes, the way it turned out has worked together for the greater good. The story is one which is directed immediately and powerfully to the frailty of our human nature. We, too, carry within ourselves a yearning love for Christ, but if we had been placed in the situation in which Peter found himself, we may not have slithered down the slippery slope of a threefold denial. Our case may have been worse. We would have taken one leap of denial and betrayal, then turned on our heels and fled the consequences with racing, cowardly heart.

What we have before us is a powerful narrative which depicts the dilemma of the human situation. A loving, impetuous man, bowed under the weight of mental turmoil and physical weariness, is suddenly attacked by a temptation in which he scarcely has the strength to think, let alone act, from the true depths of his soul.

It was a sudden, lateral attack, not from the authorities or the known enemy, but from a servant-girl and the bystanders. Wrapped around in his cloak, perhaps taking refuge in the shade of a pillar as the flames caused shadows to dance around the walls, he suddenly felt the eyes of the servant-girl upon him, "You also were with Jesus, the man from Nazareth."

And there the denial began. First, he said he did not understand, then he denied that he had been with Jesus, then he began to curse and swore an oath, "I do not know this man you are talking about."

Once the denial had begun there was no stopping it—and Peter suddenly realized that he could hear the second cockcrow, and the words of Jesus came flooding back, "Before the cock crows twice, you will deny me three times." And the narrative reveals the true Peter—"And he broke down and wept."

Prayer

Jesus, denied by those who love you: I stand in Peter's place, having made my emotional affirmations of loyalty and devotion and having denied you by my words and my silences. Sorrow, grief, and repentance were the way back for Peter. So let me take the same path, finding forgiveness and restoration by your grace. Then deliver me from future cowardice; let me stand for righteousness wherever evil is perpetuated.

Reflection

Jesus is handed over, denied, and abused wherever human beings suffer. You may not have been directly responsible for such suffering in our own or other parts of the world, but indirectly and, by silence and indifference, Christ is frequently denied. Take up today's international news and see where your stand, your influence, your contribution, can make a difference to one soul, or in one place.

Lent 3

—✠—

Judas, the Traitor

LENT 3: SUNDAY

Judas, Who Betrayed Him

Then Jesus summoned his twelve disciples and gave them authority over unclean spirits, to cast them out, and to cure every disease
and every sickness. These are the names of the twelve apostles:
first, Simon, also known as Peter, and his brother Andrew; James
son of Zebedee, and his brother John; Philip and Bartholomew;
Thomas and Matthew the tax collector; James son of Alphaeus, and
Thaddaeus; Simon the Cananaean, and Judas Iscariot, the one who
betrayed him.

MATTHEW 10:1–4

I was startled, as a boy, when I heard an eloquent Welsh preacher
begin his sermon like this: "I've never heard of a dog called Judas."
The comment did not originate with him, but it struck me with some
force.

During this week we shall be thinking much about this poor man.
He carries a kind of curse around with him, as if he were bearing the
mark of Cain, or the beast nature of Caliban, or what seems to many
Franciscans to be the deviousness of Brother Elias within the early
circle of those who surrounded Saint Francis. Poor Judas.

And of course it wasn't just Judas. The malignant powers of darkness were at work within and outside the circle of the disciples. Satanic power was pursuing the Prince of Peace to death, and so many
were caught up in the conflict, both in Church and state.

But in this man, Judas Iscariot, there is particular and clear attention drawn to his tragedy in the drama of the passion and death of
Jesus, encapsulated in the words, "The devil had…put it into the heart
of Judas…to betray him" (Jn 13:2).

This sounds all the more strange when today's passage opens with
Jesus giving his twelve disciples authority over evil spirits as part of
their healing ministry. Could Judas have stood against the powers of
darkness in the name of Christ, cast them out by his authority, and

then, at the last, allow himself to be possessed by the demonic power that betrayed Jesus to his death? Can there be, as Paul Bunyan said, a door to hell from the very gate of heaven?

If so, we need all the more to realize that our salvation and our holiness are gifts of grace, and not of our merit and ability. The counsel is sound: "If you think you are standing, watch out that you do not fall" (1 Cor 10:12). The apostle Paul understood this well enough when he wrote, "I punish my body and enslave it, so that after proclaiming to others I myself should not be disqualified" (1 Cor 9:27).

Look at the apostolic list. They are all very different. Can you imagine any other group composed of a quisling like Matthew, who let himself be used in the hands of the occupying power for the collection of taxes, set next to Simon the Zealot, who in other circumstances would have gone to any lengths, including assassination, for the patriotic, national cause of Israel. And here was Judas. He was different from the others in a number ways. He came from Kerioth, a village in the south of Judea, and that itself made him stand out.

I saw a psychological profile of the disciples recently, and it went through the Twelve, showing that none of them were really psychologically fit and reliable to fulfill the roles of leaders, teachers, organizers, ambassadors, PR men—except Judas. He seemed to fit into all the right management, religious, and psychological categories necessary. This made me wonder about Church leaders generally. I remember filling in my application for theological training and ordination. Some of the questions concerned my psychological suitability for the task. I had the cheekiness to ask, in the covering letter, if Ezekiel or the apostle Paul would have been accepted. But Judas was chosen by Jesus.

This question of being chosen was a selective act that took out the Twelve from among the wider circle of followers, and the question arises whether Jesus saw the deterioration which would overtake Judas, as he saw the potential for good in a man like Peter.

The element of choice is important here, for as Jesus chose Peter and Judas, so they chose Jesus, and could keep on choosing. We must avoid any dark notions of double predestination, for there have been times in the history of the Church when people have thought that God, in some hidden, eternal counsel, predestined an elect number to salvation, and not stopping there, also predestined the majority of his human creation to eternal damnation. This dark theology of double predestination goes together with notions of inquisitions and the torture of the human body for the salvation of the soul—doctrines that come from darkness, rather than light.

It is important to note that Luke, in his parallel account, does not say, "Judas, who betrayed him," but "Judas Iscariot, who became a traitor" (6:16). The Twelve all *become* disciples, and the "becoming" was a process of discipleship, which means learning. "Becoming" can go either way. One can become holy or become evil, and we are all constantly moving in one or the other direction.

When Jesus chose Judas, and Judas chose Jesus, there was the potential for good all round. Jesus, in the center of his being (what we call ontologically), was without the warp and twist in human nature that theologians call "original sin," and yet he needed to move dynamically (what we call existentially) towards a maturity in love and suffering in his humanity. The disciples were caught up in sinfulness. They, like us, were deficient in their human nature, affected by the alienation which is part of the whole human race. Therefore, the dynamic movement of discipleship had to begin with forgiveness and reconciliation, and move on into holiness, compassion, and love. This is what their discipleship was all about. But Judas got stuck at some point in the process.

Notice I use the words *point* and *process*, for it is frequently both. Certainly the process is obvious, even in our seven days' study of him. But there may well have been a point, a moment, a decisive act of will in some confrontation with wicked men or with the powers of darkness, in which he opened his mind and heart to evil, and Satan entered in. We shall see where it led.

Prayer

Jesus, who ordained the Twelve: I have felt your call, responded to your grace, and desire to be your disciple. The die was cast in my decision to follow you; let the process of sanctification continue. Deliver me from my own fallenness and from the powers of darkness, and keep me in your love.

Reflection

Look first into your own heart's experience, and then around you at your friends, acquaintances, and neighbors. All of us are in the process of dynamic movement towards, or away from love. Seek in your life today to draw a little closer to the Savior, and seek that your influence may enable your neighbor to do the same.

LENT 3: MONDAY

He Was a Thief

Six days before the Passover Jesus came to Bethany, the home of Lazarus, whom he had raised from the dead. There they gave a dinner for him. Martha served, and Lazarus was one of those at the table with him. Mary took a pound of costly perfume made of pure nard, anointed Jesus' feet, and wiped them with her hair. The house was filled with the fragrance of the perfume. But Judas Iscariot, one of his disciples (the one who was about to betray him), said, "Why was this perfume not sold for three hundred denarii and the money given to the poor?" (He said this not because he cared about the poor, but because he was a thief; he kept the common purse and used to steal what was put into it.) Jesus said, "Leave her alone. She bought it so that she might keep it for the day of my burial. You always have the poor with you, but you do not always have me."

JOHN 12:1–8

Into this very beautiful yet sorrowful scene a strident, discordant note is sounded by Judas. It indicates a process of movement along a scale with hatred at one extreme and love at the other.

To be a disciple of Jesus meant to be taken up into the dynamic process of positive, forward movement, leaving behind the egocentric desires of the old life, and growing into maturity and love. In Judas' case, the movement was backward and negative.

Jesus showed great courage in appearing publicly in Bethany at this Passover time, for the previous chapter tells us that the authorities had outlawed him: "The chief priests and the Pharisees had given orders that anyone who knew where Jesus was should let them know, so that they might arrest him" (11:57).

Yet here he was, exposed and vulnerable, at one and the same time the object of love and scorn from different directions. In this very house at Bethany the different attitudes of the characters are displayed, and we may well find ourselves among them.

Martha was serving; Lazarus was sharing; Mary was adoring;

Judas was complaining. They were all involved in this process of dynamic movement, for none of us stands still in life. We have to move backwards or forwards, not only in our great decisions, but in the simple actions of ordinary living.

The action that became the center of attention was that of Mary kneeling at the feet of Jesus, anointing them with the expensive ointment of pure nard, and wiping them with her unbound hair. This was a dramatic action, beautiful in the eyes of Jesus, remarkable in the eyes of the onlookers, but disreputable, displeasing, and discomforting in the eyes of Judas.

The consequence of this action was twofold: the whole house was filled with the fragrance of the perfumed ointment, and a duplicitous and grating challenge was voiced by Judas.

Commentators have seen in the rising fragrance from this devotional act of Mary a symbol of the loving and reconciling gospel spreading throughout the Church and the world. In the other versions of this story, Jesus says, "Wherever this good news is proclaimed in the whole world, what she has done will be told in remembrance of her" (Mt 26:13; Mk 14:9).

As I was writing this chapter I had a visit from Judith, who was a student at Glasgow University when I was chaplain there twenty-five years ago. She experienced perplexities about her faith then and has encountered difficulties along the path since. But we have kept in touch, and she has known that the grace of the Lord has followed her each step of the way. This visit, with Peter, her husband, was an occasion of great rejoicing, for they have both recently become tertiaries (Third Order members) of our Society of Saint Francis, and wanted to express their joy.

Judith brought me a gift to mark the occasion, and it was one which I hoped someone would give me this Christmas: some vials of aromatherapy essential oils, especially frankincense and myrrh, to burn in my makeshift chapel during Eucharist and the praying of the Liturgy of the Hours. And with the oils there was a small container of aromatherapy ointment of tea tree, lavender, and eucalyptus essential oils.

When I tried it yesterday, the chapel was filled with its fragrance, and I was moved almost to tears because of the symbolism of our friendship through the years, and because I was engaged in writing this chapter, where the house was filled with the fragrance of Mary's offering, indicating her penitence and adoration.

I've just opened and touched the ointment again during these sentences, and its pure beauty fills the air as I resolve to read this Scripture passage at Matins this morning, and to write to Judith and Peter later today to obtain their approval for the inclusion of this story.

So you see how infinitely sad is the strident complaint, the duplicitous challenge, the discordant note of criticism which Judas introduced into the atmosphere of table fellowship, penitence, and adoration. It is not an accident that the love of Christ and the things of God possess a savor, a fragrance of sweetness, while the dark things of Satan have the smell of corruption and decay (2 Cor 2:14–16; Eph 5:2).

When a man or woman frequently indulges in negative criticism, sarcasm, and cynicism (here again is the slippery slope), it is a reflection of their own interior problems and immaturity. Judas was called to be a saint, ordained to holiness and love. But a sad process of deterioration was taking place in his soul. Perhaps it was brought on by a moment of temptation, a sowing of lust for power, a corrupting influence in relationship, or even by an exposure to handling of money, for he was treasurer of the apostolic band. The commentator B. F. Westcott says that temptation often comes through that for which we are naturally fitted—and our passage says that Judas became a thief.

He was disconcerted by the sight of this woman with unbound hair (it seems that Judas had a strict code of public morals) displaying such overt emotional sorrow and love down at Jesus' feet—and did not like the fragrance of it all.

The image of the devotee at the feet of the Master is a universal one, but one which Judas was not able to understand. It need not have been like that, but had become so. The gradual process of decay and corruption was active, and Judas covered it with a duplicitous concern for the poor.

There was no doubt about Jesus' option for the poor, but here and now was the time for penitence, adoration, and a costly outpouring of devotion. As Jesus said, "You always have the poor with you, but you do not always have me."

Prayer

Jesus anointed at Bethany: I find myself present in this company today. With Martha I desire to serve you; with Lazarus to sit at table with you; with Mary to kneel at your feet in costly devotion. Can it be true that with Judas I discover within myself a carping spirit of criticism, sarcasm, and, at times, cynicism towards others, towards myself? Arrest any process of deterioration and corruption in my soul, Lord, for I realize that only by your grace can such a deliverance be effected, and I want to rely on that grace today.

Reflection

This identification of ourselves with the characters in the story is the pattern of our sharing. Does it help you today to see in yourself a strange mixture of devotion and duplicity? Perhaps this is a stage in the process of your journey towards holiness. So let it do its work.

LENT 3: TUESDAY

What Will You Give Me?

The chief priests and the scribes were looking for a way to put Jesus to death, for they were afraid of the people. Then Satan entered into Judas called Iscariot, who was one of the twelve; he went away and conferred with the chief priests and officers of the temple police about how he might betray him to them. They were greatly pleased and agreed to give him money. So he consented and began to look for an opportunity to betray him to them when no crowd was present.

LUKE 22:2–6

We sometimes sing the words: "What can I give him, poor as I am...." But one version of today's passage has Judas asking, "What will you give me...?" (Mt 26:15). Can it really be true that a simple and basic avarice was at the bottom of Judas' betrayal of Christ?

I don't think it was as clear as that. There are hints and implications in the Gospel narratives upon which too much has been built, and we shall survey some of the possible motivations in Saturday's meditation. Yet the money factor looms large, though it seems to be a symptom of Judas' degeneration, and not the prime cause.

Whatever importance that or other factors may have, we are dealing, in these chapters, with the powers of darkness which are now concentrating upon the delivering up of Jesus to the authorities to be done away with once and for all. Luke and John are quite explicit about the demonic element, and (remembering that the epistles were written before the gospels) we should notice that the apostle Paul said that demonic forces were the ultimate agents in crucifying the Lord of Glory (1 Cor 2:8). Also, after Jesus' temptation in the wilderness, we read that "when the devil had finished every test, he departed from him until an opportune time" (Lk 4:13). This is the time.

Yet we are not to think of Judas as a predestined pawn in some cosmic game, but remember that he chose his path. We shall see that Jesus made an appeal to him at the Last Supper and even in his final word in Gethsemane—to no avail. It makes us realize that a person can come into direct contact with Jesus, see his miracles, feel his compassion, begin to walk in his way—and then repudiate him. The other side of this dark observation is the wonder that choice is before us. God will not coerce us, for there is something about human freedom that is exceedingly precious. If we cheapen it by our false choices, we may betray ourselves and find at last that we have fallen into a pit that we ourselves have dug.

Even if we think that the money was only part of Judas' problem, we can see that this passage portrays him already caught up in the web of deceit; already enmeshed in the machinations of the authorities. Or to use yet another metaphor, the wheels of the deadly process are already turning.

When we read of this secret assignation, we wonder if this was its beginning or whether someone had already sought out Judas. Then the question arises: What exactly did Judas do? What was the nature of his betrayal? We can say that he identified Jesus. Whereas Peter said, "I do *not* know him," Judas said, "I *do* know him," and both, in their turn, were betrayals of Jesus. Then Judas identified *where* Jesus would be at a specified time. We wonder if he also communicated inside information as to Jesus' claim to be Messiah. Jesus kept a certain confidence within the apostolic circle about this, because he was not the kind of Messiah that the nationalistic Jews sought or expected. At the last, Judas actually led the authorities and temple police to Jesus in Gethsemane, and actually "handed him over"—which is the meaning of his betrayal.

What Judas did not do was to appear at the trial or give witness against Jesus. Perhaps he could not have done that. Following on from what we have said about human choice, it seems that Judas made little choices on the road that paved the way to that awful decision to go to the authorities and commit himself. All three Synoptic Gospels say that as a result of their conference, Judas, from that moment, sought an opportunity to betray him. And the opportunity certainly came.

Up until then, perhaps it could have been avoided. But this conference certainly seems to have been a watershed decision and action, though perhaps inevitable because he had assented to the corrupting process of compromise, deceit, and double-dealing along the way.

Just imagine if he could have found repentance at any point in the journey, and called upon the grace of God. Even if this had happened after the betrayal, the same mercy and grace would have sped him into the midst of the judging Sanhedrin with his confession of guilt, and cry of repentance. Jesus would have pardoned him, for he still loved him, and Judas would have gone to a glorious martyr's death with his Savior, instead of alone to an ignominious death, and the reputation of the arch-betrayer. For this act, Dante placed Judas in the lowest hell of cold and ice, prepared for calculating, deliberate betrayers of love, and not for hot sinners, swept away in a river of passion.

All these "supposing" and "might have been" observations do not change the facts, for they are part of that story. But what of our story? We are still on the way, and we are thankfully in the position of evaluating where we stand. Questions about the deterioration or positive maturation of our lives are open and vital to us now. We have the freedom to choose, and the opportunity to repent and call for grace to change.

This passage freezes Judas in that act of conferring with the authorities, which was a watershed decision for him. A consideration of that very action could be an opportune moment for us.

Prayer

Jesus, friend of sinners: You did not cease to love Judas, even as you were aware of his duplicity and betrayal. Your love for him and for me is freely offered at every point along the way; grant me grace to make constant decisions of integrity; keep me in the path of honesty, simplicity and openness towards you, and towards my fellows.

Reflection

It becomes clearer that those who are faithful in small things are faithful in the greater places of choice and opportunity. Can you trace, in your life, both deterioration and maturity, as you have lost sight of love, and then regained it and been faithful? Take every opportunity to strengthen integrity, honesty, simplicity, so that you will not at last be betrayed yourself, or betray others.

LENT 3: WEDNESDAY

Surely Not I, Rabbi?

When it was evening, he took his place with the twelve; and while they were eating, he said, "Truly I tell you, one of you will betray me." And they became greatly distressed and began to say to him one after another, "Surely not I, Lord?" He answered, "The one who has dipped his hand into the bowl with me will betray me. The Son of Man goes as it is written of him, but woe to that one by whom the Son of Man is betrayed! It would have been better for that one not to have been born." Judas, who betrayed him, said, "Surely not I, Rabbi?" He replied, "You have said so."

MATTHEW 26:20–25

At what point could Judas have turned back? Was there a moment at which he was beyond redemption? Even if Christ's mercy is infinite, was there the possibility that Judas (and thus everyone) had himself made it impossible to turn around, to repent, to start again?

We use the word *companion* for those who link themselves with our Franciscan Order in the family of love and prayer. The word means "eating bread together," and this was the case as the disciples reclined with Jesus at the Last Supper. It should have been a time of remembering the goodness and mercy of God in the past, gaining strength and joy in bread and wine, and going forward into the blessedness of doing God's will.

But here, at this supper, the shadow of the cross had fallen on each of them. For when Jesus said, "One of you shall betray me," the disciples all fell into grief and distress, and asked, "Is it I, Lord?"

These words can be interpreted in two ways. Was each of the disciples saying, "I wonder if it could be me?"—in the realization that the human heart is full of duplicity, hypocrisy, and double-dealing, even in the most sacred things, and in loving relationships. In John's Gospel (13:18), Jesus quotes the prophetic psalm of treachery in love with immense sadness, "Even my bosom friend in whom I trusted, who ate of my bread, has lifted the heel against me" (41:9). The disciples may have asked their question realizing their own vulnerability and potential for failure as the shadows deepened and the coming storm was inevitable.

The other way of understanding the question is reflected in most translations as: "Surely not I, Lord?" There may even be an oblique accusation of neighbor in the words, with the belief, or determination, that the speaker would not be the one to betray. And yet they all did betray Jesus. Judas' response differs from the others' in one word. Whereas they said "Lord," he said "Rabbi." Even here, perhaps unconsciously, Judas places the relationship on the level of instruction instead of relationship, and this may well be the reason why many churchgoers will accept Jesus as an Example, but do not understand their relationship to him as Savior, Beloved, and Lord. There are twelve disciples here, but it seems in this narrative as if it is only Judas and Jesus. And we are drawn into the intensity of the moment.

Judas had been secretly plotting, and none of the disciples seemed to have any idea of what was really going on. But Jesus knew. It was not that Judas gave himself away by a look, a mannerism, an attitude of guilt, but that Jesus knew what was in the human heart—and especially in Judas' heart at this time.

There are moments in the wider narrative when Jesus seems to say, "Judas, even now turn away from this evil, turn to me in sorrow, for I love you...." We shall capture another such moment in Gethsemane. But here as a companion, dipping in the same dish, hands touching, eyes meeting, hearts exposed, Jesus confronts Judas with two things: the enormity of his sin, and the facing of himself in his own heart.

This is always Jesus' way—the path of suffering love. He could have blasted Judas, paralyzed his will, violently broken his resolve, caused the political strategy to have collapsed about his ears. But he would not. How precious to God is human freedom.

He says to Judas, in effect, "Judas, look at *what* you are doing. Can you go on with it? Can you betray at such depth, can you be so treacherous to me who has always loved you and will continue to love you?" The other side of that is Jesus' awful words, "Woe to that one by whom the Son of Man is betrayed. It would have been better for that one not to have been born."

The second thing Jesus does is to face Judas with himself, as if to say, "Judas, you must not only look at what you are doing, and who you are betraying, but gaze deep into your soul and ask if that is what you were meant for. I called you to love; I ordained you to serve me in holiness. You need me for the fulfillment of your life, and to turn away from me is to turn to disintegration and ultimate despair." If these weapons fail—if Judas can resist such grace, then he chooses for himself to go out into the darkness.

When Judas asked his question, "Surely not I, Rabbi?" Jesus replied gently and sorrowfully, "You have said so." In other words, Jesus is laying the responsibility, the possibility of turning back, the decision as to the outcome, squarely upon Judas himself, while always longing for his return, desiring his love and going forward to accomplish for him the redemption that only he can bring about. Each refusal is accepted for the present, but the final word will be with Christ—and that word is always love.

Prayer

Jesus, who knows the human heart: Give me today knowledge of what I am accomplishing in my life; give me understanding of my true self. In the mirror of your word I realize my own potential for failure and duplicity, but I also feel the exhilarating call of your Spirit. Let me learn today, and give me the grace to always turn from evil, always to turn to you for mercy, and to be one of your true companions in the breaking of bread.

Reflection

Today's passage opens up more of the nature of God in Christ, and the potential for good and evil in the human personality. It is clear that Judas, in betraying Christ, is really betraying himself. We should link more closely the understanding and doing the will of God with our own peace of mind, maturity, and fulfillment.

LENT 3: THURSDAY

Betrayed With a Kiss

While he [Jesus] was still speaking, Judas, one of the twelve, arrived; with him was a large crowd with swords and clubs, from the chief priests and elders of the people. Now the betrayer had given them a sign, saying, "The one I will kiss is the man; arrest him." At once he came up to Jesus and said, "Greetings, Rabbi" and kissed him. Jesus said to him, "Friend, do what you are here to do." Then they came and laid hands on Jesus and arrested him.

MATTHEW 26:47–50 (SEE ALSO LUKE 22:48)

In the garden of Gethsemane, Jesus had entered into a full understanding of the dark abyss that lay before him, embracing the will of God towards suffering and death. The three disciples had slept their sleep of grief and exhaustion, failing to watch with him in that most important hour. At that moment Jesus roused them for the last time with the fearful words, "See, the hour is at hand, and the Son of Man is betrayed into the hands of sinners....See, my betrayer is at hand."

Whether he saw, or foresaw, Judas leading the Sanhedrin, the temple police, and the rabble, the hour had come. And how they came—a crowd with swords and clubs, with terror and violence. And John adds, "with lanterns and torches" (18:3). Did they expect Jesus to be hiding in the shadows of rocks and bushes? Did they expect to be confronted with an armed band who would defend him to the death? Neither of these options were in Jesus' mind. In the midst of the confusion, noise and clanging of the crowd, the cold sweat of perplexity and fear of the disciples, Jesus steps forward. He is quiet, firm, courageous—a pool of tranquillity amidst the trampling of angry feet, the cry of bloodthirsty men, and the cold, calculating determination of the Sanhedrin—led by Judas.

And what does Judas do? Acting according to plan, he drew near to Jesus and kissed him, saying, "Greetings, Rabbi." That would not have been unusual if he had come as a disciple to his master—but this was a kiss of betrayal.

Jesus' response varies in the telling. Luke reports Jesus as saying, "Judas, is it with a kiss that you are betraying the Son of Man?" (22:48). Our passage reports the words, "Friend, do what you are here to do." In both cases there is a confrontational meeting in which only Judas and Jesus exist—a brief moment encapsulating eternity. And there are two elements in it. There is the last, yearning plea of Jesus contained in the words, "Judas" and "Friend." But there follows the words which are neither a question nor a reproach, but a call now to clear action. If it is to begin, then let it be.

It is Jesus in command here, at the very moment when he submits himself, allows himself to be "handed over" (which is the meaning of the Greek word for betrayal). But from here on he surrenders to a passivity in which he is acted upon, and enters into the meaning of his Gethsemane words, "Your will be done."

At last the disciples understand what is happening, though ignorant of the deeper meaning. Judas is now out in the open—it all becomes clear. But to their minds there are only two options—to fight or to run. Neither of these was Jesus' way, and our passage leads on to Jesus' rebuke of the disciple who drew a hidden sword in fear and defense, and cut off the ear of the high priest's servant, "Put your sword back into its place; for all who take the sword will perish by the sword" (verse 52). As Jesus would soon say to Pilate, "If my kingdom were from this world, my followers would be fighting to keep me from being handed over to the Jews" (Jn 18:36).

The conflict was not to do with physical violence or worldly politics. There were deeper malignant powers at work, and the disciples had not yet learned that only the spiritual weapons of truth and love were effective against the demonic darkness that sought the death of the Prince of Peace (see Lk 22:53).

Here, on the nether side of the passion of Jesus, the disciples could only fight or run, but on the other side of Easter we shall see things as Jesus saw them in Gethsemane. The apostle Paul later saw it clearly: "Our struggle is not against enemies of blood and flesh, but against the rulers, against the authorities, against the cosmic powers of this present darkness, against the spiritual forces of evil in the heavenly places" (Eph 6:12).

Jesus meets violence with compassion and healing as he intervenes in the scuffle and turns to the injured servant: "'No more of this!' and he touched his ear and healed him" (Lk 22:51).

In his perceptive book, *The Stature of Waiting,* W. H. Vanstone's thesis is that up until this episode Jesus was in control, set the agenda, took the initiative. But in Gethsemane he yielded himself in complete surrender to the will of God, and at the arrest he allowed himself to be "handed over" and gave himself up to the cross for our redemption.

The pattern is a divine one, and there comes a time in the life of the disciple of Jesus when he or she realizes that there is no other way into the deep places of prayer and of love but to allow this pattern to repeat itself by the Holy Spirit in his or her life.

Look at the scene again. There is a turbulent rabble, provoking terror and fear; there is the Sanhedrin made up of calculating chief priests, scribes, and elders, and assisted by the violent temple police ready to take Jesus by force.

Judas led them all into the midst of the perplexed and fearful disciples, and singled out the Savior with a kiss of betrayal. And Jesus stands in the midst of them in a sorrowful but regal serenity, reminding us of the words of Saint Teresa of Ávila:

> *Let nothing disturb you,*
> *Nothing affright you,*
> *All things are passing,*
> *God never changes.*
> *Patient endurance*
> *Attains to all things;*
> *Who God possesses*
> *In nothing is wanting.*
> *Alone God suffices.*

"Then all the disciples deserted him, and fled" (verse 56).

Prayer

Jesus, betrayed with a kiss: When all things go well I am your disciple; when others approve, I am willing to be counted among those who follow you. But when darkness comes, when voices are raised against you, when my witness would lead to rejection, violence, and even death, then by silence or by the betrayer's kiss I am capable of deserting you. Have mercy on me now, Lord, so that in the time of trial I may be faithful.

Reflection

Do you see the difference between the understanding and attitude of the disciples in Gethsemane and a post-Easter faith? Have you asked yourself where you stand in relation to the value of the Christ who is rejected, abused, and done to death? Can you see, even here in the garden, that there are creative powers of love which are deeper still than the powers of darkness, and that will at last vindicate the way of healing compassion and give the victory to love?

—— ✚ ——

LENT 3: FRIDAY

I Have Sinned

When Judas, his betrayer, saw that Jesus was condemned, he repented and brought back the thirty pieces of silver to the chief priests
and the elders. He said, "I have sinned by betraying innocent blood."
But they said, "What is that to us? See to it yourself." Throwing
down the pieces of silver in the temple, he departed; and he went
and hanged himself. But the chief priests, taking the pieces of silver, said, "It is not lawful to put them into the treasury, since they
are blood money." After conferring together, they used them to buy
the potter's field as a place to bury foreigners. For this reason that
field has been called the Field of Blood to this day. Then was fulfilled what had been spoken through the prophet Jeremiah, "And
they took the thirty pieces of silver, the price of the one on whom a
price had been set…and they gave them for the potter's field."

MATTHEW 27:3–10

W hat did Judas do once the authorities had taken Jesus into their
hands? He seemed not to have accompanied them. Certainly
he did not appear at the trial or bear witness against Jesus. This seems
strange, for substantial witnesses were needed. The ones who had been
put up to it were contradicting themselves (Mk 14:55–56).

But strange things were taking place within Judas himself. He
had been so busy, so secretive, so taken up with the external events.
And now it was all over, and it began to dawn upon him that he had
done something powerfully significant, something world-changing,
something terrible. So the focus of attention was turned within.

From the moment the authorities departed with Jesus, the rabble
dispersed and the disciples fled, he was left alone—and alone as he
had never been in his life before. It was not simply that he was without company, but that his soul began to taste the darkness of a lonely
night that would encompass and suffocate his very being (Jn 13:30).

There is a legend that tells of Judas wandering in hopeless frenzy
through the night, until in the early hours he comes across a group of

workmen fashioning a cross. This brought home to him the horror of what he had done, the grim reality of torture, suffering, and agony that would be the result of his calculated planning and awful action.

However it came about, our passage opens with the words which cause us to pause in our condemnation of Judas, and to think through the happenings again. We read that Judas saw, repented, confessed, returned, and acted.

I was brought up to believe that the difference between Peter and Judas was that Peter *denied* but Judas *betrayed*, and that Peter's act led to *repentance* but Judas's to *remorse*. Therefore Peter was saved but Judas was damned.

Over the years, reading the narrative continually, and living my life's experience in the arena of faith and of the world, I have often had reason to think again about so many things. It is easy to think and live superficially, and to take over other people's opinions and faith, and think they are your own. It may be that Judas only "repented himself" and was filled with a terrible remorse that his plans had gone wrong, and that the same demonic power that drove him to betray now caused him to rush to a madman's death and into eternal darkness.

But before we come to such a conclusion, let's look at the text again. Judas saw what he had done. The condemnation of Jesus seems to have been an amazing revelation to him, so we must ask why that should be. Then Judas *repented*. What does this mean? It is not the word *metanoia*, but the lighter word *metamelomai*, but literally it does mean "change what one has at heart." There is certainly remorse here, but it has an affective meaning, not simply Judas' mind, but his heart, so it seems that he is not entirely given to evil.

Then Judas *confessed*—and what a confession that was. "I have sinned by betraying innocent blood." This is a cry wrung from the heart, and it reverberates down to our own day. It is a cry of repentance from the hearts of all who have done wrong, often committed terrible atrocities—but conscience and sorrow mingle in the awful realization of acts of violence and unlove that lead to sorrow, pain, and death. We cannot minimize the terrible thing that Judas did—the betraying and handing over to evil of the very Son of Love, the Prince of Peace. But he repented and confessed his sin.

He had no pity, mercy, or understanding from the callous priests and elders. All they were concerned with was their own skin, their own position of power, and the maintaining of the establishment status quo.

If the other disciples had gathered together somehow, in sorrow and misery, and Judas had confessed to them, he may not have been met with such callousness, but he may well have been utterly condemned and perhaps even killed by them, in spite of the fact that they had all abandoned Jesus in Gethsemane.

But what if he had confessed to Jesus, or if he could not have found his way to him, what if he had thrown himself down at the place where Jesus had prayed in Gethsemane, and confessed to God in utter, abandoned helplessness, and thrown himself upon the mercy and judgment of God? Perhaps he would have found pardon.

Then we read that after his rejected confession he *acted*. He did two things. First, he threw down the silver pieces in the temple. At least he *tried* to get rid of some of the consequences of his sin. It was to no avail, but he did try. It is a terrible thing when we have done something so terrible, offended love so greatly, betrayed a loved one so radically, so cruelly, so finally, that we cannot turn the clock back, put things right, atone, or make amends. We cry, "If only…" or "I didn't mean to say that…to do that…." When love is lost, the world becomes empty, life meaningless, and existence of no value. It struck me again the other day when I heard the beautifully melancholic song "We seem like passing strangers now…" by Billy Eckstein and Sarah Vaughan.

The second thing Judas did was to commit suicide. Matthew's narrative says he went out and hanged himself. There seemed nothing else to do but to end it all. He did not live on his avaricious gain; he did not set himself up in business giving false weights; he did not visit the temple in his later years saying hypocritical prayers and paying lip service to it all. He knew what he had done. And he repented. Is there mercy for him?

Prayer

Jesus, Savior of Judas: You are Savior to me. I cannot read Judas' heart, but I know a little of my own. I see there is more beneath the surface of the story than I had imagined, and there is more to my heart's motives than I can yet understand. My prayer today is, "Lord, have mercy upon Judas. Lord, have mercy upon me."

Reflection

Consider how quick we often are in criticizing and condemning others whose sins are not according to our inclinations or temptations. Recognize how often the stories of those who have sinned in our society are also the victims of that society. Without excusing the reality of sin or the responsibility of the perpetrators of cruelty and evil, let our compassion be first for the victims, and then for the perpetrators. For only God knows the whole truth, and he alone is the righteous Judge.

—— ✠ ——

LENT 3: SATURDAY

Saved or Damned?

In those days Peter stood among the believers (together the crowd numbered about one hundred and twenty persons) and said, "Friends, the Scripture had to be fulfilled, which the Holy Spirit through David foretold concerning Judas, who became a guide for those who arrested Jesus—for he was numbered among us and was allotted his share in this ministry." (Now this man acquired a field with the reward of his wickedness; and falling headlong, he burst open in the middle and all his bowels gushed out. This become known to all the residents of Jerusalem, so that the field was called in their language Hakeldama, that is, Field of Blood). For it is written in the book of Psalms, "Let his homestead become desolate, and let there be no one to live in it"; and "Let another take his position of overseer."

ACTS 1:15–20 (SEE ALSO VERSE 25)

I have just finished writing yesterday's meditation on Judas with great heaviness of heart. Part of the reason is my involvement with the text in the context of prayer, because I have been writing these Judas meditations after my early period of prayer, beginning the writing soon after 6:00 A.M. in my hermitage, surrounded by the winter darkness of Advent.

So we come to the final consideration, and I realize that the question "saved or damned?" is not ours to make, but lies within the mercy of God. I am not endeavoring to change anyone's mind, but to share with you my own reflections, and to consider again the dilemma and shame, the wonder and glory of our humanity portrayed in Judas and Jesus.

I am not concerned here with Luke's story in terms of its differences from Matthew's. It may be that poor Judas, in hanging himself from some tree branch, fell headlong from there with the nauseating results indicated in today's passage. Or perhaps Luke's story comes from a different tradition. What we are concerned with here is not textual criticism but the realities of life and death, of salvation and damnation. Perhaps Judas was both damned and saved. What I mean by that is that he was certainly responsible for what he did, and therefore his interior remorse and the whole narrative of repentance spoken of yesterday carried him into tasting interiorly the judgment of God upon all the unloving. But perhaps also he was saved—for if only damnation follows sin, where are any of us?

Attitudes to Judas are found on a wide spectrum, from the sentimental to the fatalistic. To illustrate these, one writer has described the sorrow of Judas as so great that he hung himself in order that his soul should hurry immediately into the next world, to fall at the feet of Jesus and plead for forgiveness. And others have maintained that Judas was a predestined pawn in the whole game, so that he was damned from all eternity and programmed to act as he did. The conclusions of such people say more about them than about Judas, and perhaps that is so for all of us.

Judas was a Judean while the other disciples were Galileans. He was one of the more discerning among them, and surely saw increasingly what kind of messiah Jesus was. If he was, like many other Judeans, nationalistic and patriotic, with a mixture of personal ambition, he may have been disappointed and disillusioned. Perhaps he did not want a suffering servant-king but a conquering hero—a victorious messiah claiming territory, power, and political influence—so he betrayed Jesus to death.

Or he may have seen Jesus as a reluctant messiah who needed to be pushed, forced, catapulted into a crisis which would compel him to show his hand, so he organized the whole scenario to push Jesus into manifesting his charismatic messianic powers, calling into action the many zealots who were waiting for such a man and for such a moment.

Again, Judas may have engineered the arrest in order to protect Jesus from an assassin's hand, or to prevent Jesus and the disciples from provoking a premature, stupid, and futile bloody insurrection which would come to nothing.

Some have even thought that Judas, realizing that the shadow of death hung over them all because of Jesus' actions, simply punted, betraying Jesus in cowardice, and ingratiating himself with the authorities in order to save his own miserable skin.

But what about the satanic influence in the story? Traditionally, Judas has been thought of as a scheming, ambitious thief, tempted by money and power, secretly profiting from the common purse and yielding at last to a financial transaction. Both Luke (22:3) and John (13:27) say that "Satan entered into Judas."

The human heart may welcome the Holy Spirit and be indwelt by love and compassion, but it may also open itself to the dimension of demonic influence and possession. This malignant power is at work at the center of the apostolic band, corrupting discipleship and fulfilling the prophetic word of betrayal (Ps 41:9).

How terrible are the words of Jesus about Judas, but they must be applied at a deeper level to all those who allow themselves to be possessed by malignant evil, "The Son of Man goes as it is written of him, but woe to that one by whom the Son of Man is betrayed. It would have been better for that one not to have been born" (Mk 14:21).

This raises an immense question. Are there people in our world about whom it can be said that it were better that they had never seen the light of day? We can think of the great tyrants of history, none worse than some of those of the last century like Stalin, responsible for tens of millions of Soviet citizens being sent to torture and death under his regime of terror; of Hitler and six million Jews tortured and incinerated in the Holocaust. And what terror did we initiate on August 6, 1945, with the dropping of the atomic bomb on Hiroshima and later on Nagasaki?

Dark cosmic powers were at work in the ancient world, and continue to corrupt people and nations with malice and hatred. During this week we have seen that there may have been a great deal of early yearning and enthusiasm when Judas answered the call of Christ to discipleship. Even though the process of corruption seems to have overtaken him for reasons about which we can only speculate, nevertheless he did not appear at the trial, he did not witness against Jesus, and yesterday's Scripture passage spoke of sorrow, remorse, and repentance. The one question which, perhaps, remains for us is whether Judas, allowing his remorse to lead him to despair in this life and to suicide, has any place in the mercy of God.

Ultimately, we can only leave him in the hands of the all-knowing and gracious God, whose secret counsels are beyond anything we can imagine. And if we believe that Jesus Christ is the image of God among humankind, we may listen to, and apply Jesus' prayer to Judas. As he was nailed to the cross, he cried, "Father, forgive them; for they do not know what they are doing" (Lk 23:34).

Prayer

Jesus, whose mercy is infinite: I have no doubt that you called me, as you called Judas, to love and holiness; but I have much self-doubt about my ability to persevere. Only by your grace can I begin to follow; only by the anointing of your Spirit can I be kept from corruption and maintained in holiness. Therefore I praise you for past mercies, I live in present forgiveness, and look to you for future joy in the spread of your reconciling word.

Reflection

As we have searched beneath the surface of the Judas story, we may have found a reflection of ourselves, and the potential for good and ill within our motivation. We need to share our discipleship with others in soul-friendship, mutual confession and fellowship. In this way, no hidden process of corruption will take hold, and we shall walk in the light of Christ, have fellowship with one another, and it will be a blessing that we were ever born.

— ✠ —

Lent 4

—✠—

Mary, His Mother

LENT 4: SUNDAY

Annunciation: Full of Grace

In the sixth month the angel Gabriel was sent by God to a town in Galilee called Nazareth, to a virgin engaged to a man whose name was Joseph, of the house of David. The virgin's name was Mary. And he came to her and said, "Greetings, favored one! The Lord is with you." But she was much perplexed by his words and pondered what sort of greeting this might be. The angel said to her, "Do not be afraid, Mary, for you have found favor with God. And now, you will conceive in your womb and bear a son, and you will name him Jesus....Mary said to the angel, "How can this be, since I am a virgin?" The angel said to her, "The Holy Spirit will come upon you, and the power of the Most High will overshadow you; therefore the child to be born will be holy; he will be called Son of God....For nothing will be impossible with God." Then Mary said, "Here am I, the servant of the Lord; let it be with me according to your word." Then the angel departed from her.

LUKE 1:26–38

This passage is not only beautiful literature, but amazing theology. It is called the Annunciation—the proclamation of the angel Gabriel to the virgin Mary, a Jewish girl from Nazareth, that God would become incarnate in her womb. Put like that, it sounds incredible, reading back all the later understanding of the early Church. But that is just what we are dealing with here—God himself become human in Jesus.

Luke's narrative moves quickly to the heart of the matter. Gabriel comes to Nazareth, to a betrothed virgin, Mary, and says, "Greetings, favored one! The Lord is with you." Then is unfolded the whole drama in four stages.

First, there is the *awe* with which Mary gazes upon this angelic visitation. Suddenly, there burst in upon the ordinariness of her present life in Nazareth a heavenly being which has to do with the temple at Jerusalem, the holy scrolls of Scripture in the synagogue, and with the fearful dimension of that other world of prayer, mystery, and the prophetic words which have erupted in Israel's history. In ways relevant to our own cultural experience, and in the measure of our understanding and faith, God can break through into our lives as we prepare during these days of Lent. Even today.

Second, there is the *perplexity* with which Mary hears the greeting. How could she possibly be favored by God, and what were the implications of such a greeting? Gabriel stilled her first fears. But when he explained the meaning of his visit—that she would conceive a son in her womb, and call his name Jesus, Savior, and that he would not only be among the prophetic line but fulfill messianic yearnings—then her perplexity increased. She explained that she had never had physical relations with a man.

Then came the *revelation*. She would remain a virgin, she would be graciously overshadowed by the Holy Spirit, for God is the God of the impossible. Gabriel then told Mary of the miracle manifest in the barren womb of Elizabeth who was now six months pregnant, and that an even greater miracle would take place in her if she would consent to this gracious invitation.

This overshadowing is the language of gentleness, not of violence; of tenderness and courtesy by which Mary was welcomed into the ineffable mystery of God's loving scheme of redemption for the world. How could Mary possibly take it in, as awe and fear mingled with perplexity, wonder, and intuitive joy? There must have been many months of interior and unconscious preparation for this moment, for God always prepares us for his surprises. His dramatic moments of intervention are only the consequence of much quiet and inward cultivation of the heart's soil for the planting of the divine seed.

So it was with Mary, and so it is with us. The yearning movement of your heart, those inexpressible longings and unfulfilled visions which have been stored secretly since childhood—perhaps they are part of the preparation for what the Lord will reveal to you in his good time and will. For God never acts prematurely or hastily. There is a divine synchronicity of the right time and place.

All this leads up to the fourth element in this dramatic narrative—the complete *obedience* in which Mary not only cooperates, but gives herself wholly, trustingly, lovingly, to the purpose of God.

What an act of obedience this is. It embraces the fullness of faith, and is greater than the faith and obedience of Abraham who went forth into the unknown by the command of God (Heb 11:8). Mary is not only in the true, prophetic line, but in her will be brought to pass the ultimate fulfillment of Israel's messianic hopes, she is the obedient servant of the Lord through whom the Christ would come into the world.

As the Fathers of the Church said, *Eva* became *Ave* (Hail), as Mary reversed the disobedience of Eve, so that Christ might reverse the Fall of Adam. It is not simply personal, nor even patriotic, but cosmic and universal. The *Fiat lux* (let there be light) of God in creation is re-echoed in the *Fiat mihi* (let it be to me) of Mary, and light flooded the world.

Luke's opening chapter contains two annunciations. The first was to Zechariah the old man, for whom the message seemed too late, for the obstacle is the couple's barrenness and old age (1:5–20). The second was to Mary the peasant girl for whom the message seems to be too early, for she is a virgin.

The Holy Spirit is involved in every human birth, but here we find a special work in granting fertility to Elizabeth's womb—a manifest miracle like that accorded to Abraham's Sarah (Gen 18:9–14). But in the case of Mary, it was a miracle of new creation. Just as the Holy Spirit had overshadowed the void of creation (Gen 1:2), and then overshadowed the tabernacle, temple, and Ark of the Covenant (Ex 40:34–35), so now the overshadowing of the same Spirit was to bring about the conception of Jesus in the womb of the virgin Mary. And she said, "Here I am, the servant of the Lord; let it be with me according to your word."

Prayer

Jesus, conceived by the Holy Spirit: I stand before you, sometimes in awe and sometimes perplexity, sometimes in fear and amazement. I believe myself to be highly favored by your grace, called to bear the Christ within my heart, and invited to be the instrument and vessel of your salvation to others. May I learn the obedience and faith manifested in the Blessed Virgin Mary, and realizing in part the difficulties of the road ahead, let me say, "Here I am, the servant of the Lord; let it be with me according to your word."

Reflection

It is not for us to rush into any great schemes of our own making. God takes the initiative in his calling and equipping of his servants. He is preparing our hearts to do his will. But when he does call, be ready, and let your response be whole hearted, wholly trusting in his grace.

——✠——

LENT 4: MONDAY

Visitation: Leaping for Joy

After those days…Elizabeth conceived, and for five months she remained in seclusion.…In those days Mary set out and went with haste to a Judean town in the hill country, where she entered the house of Zechariah and greeted Elizabeth. When Elizabeth heard Mary's greeting, the child leaped in her womb. And Elizabeth was filled with the Holy Spirit and exclaimed with a loud cry, "Blessed are you among women, and blessed is the fruit of your womb. And why has this happened to me, that the mother of my Lord comes to me? For as soon as I heard the sound of your greeting, the child in my womb leaped for joy. And blessed is she who believed that there would be a fulfillment of what was spoken to her by the Lord."

LUKE 1:24, 39–56

This is a marvelous piece of writing which communicates an even more marvelous story. Leaping for joy is a consequence of being filled with the Holy Spirit. The amazing truth here, which pregnant women and mothers will understand best, is that there is something in conceiving, bearing, giving birth, which is unlike anything else in human life, and most like the activity of the Holy Spirit who is "the Lord and giver of life."

I remember, as a young pastor, going to visit Maureen in Saint David's Hospital, in Cardiff, Wales, where she had just given birth to her first baby, Helen. She was radiant and full of excitement as she told me the wonderful experience it had been, and how amazed she was because of the unexpected nature of the joy. I could only listen empathetically, but there was no doubt about the reality of the experience. And I've often wondered since what it could possibly be like to carry life within one's own body, to conceive, nurture, protect, sustain, bear, and bring to birth another human life. Amazing.

But that is only part of our narrative. Mary hurried the four miles west of Jerusalem to the hill country of Ain Karim, to confront the miracle of old Elizabeth's pregnancy.

No sooner had she crossed over the threshold and cried out a greeting, than Elizabeth was suddenly seized with the power and joy. The Holy Spirit filled her, and the unborn prophet in her womb leaped for joy—and did she *feel* it. Yes, I can *imagine* it, but what did it really *feel* like? Something quite wonderful was taking place between two women in Luke's story, both of whom were instruments and channels of God's creative love, and the electric line of communication between them was alive with power.

Something of that charismatic joy can be envisaged in the story of when the Ark of the Covenant was taken into the house of Obed-Edom of Gath for three months, and because of its presence, the house was blessed by God (2 Sam 6:11–15). When it was time for the Ark to be taken in procession to Jerusalem, David went before it, dancing with all his might in the presence of the Lord, with joy, shouting, and the sound of trumpets. One of the medieval titles of Mary was "the Ark of God," and you can see how rich is the symbolism of that title without me spelling it out.

Can we experience today something of the spiritual joy that Mary and Elizabeth felt in that house in the Judean hills? A few months ago I had a letter from Ron Crahart whom I had not seen since we were both twenty—forty years ago. He picked up a book of mine, not knowing me by my Franciscan name Ramon, but attracted by the title, *A Hidden Fire.*

As he read, there was rekindled in his heart that "old time religion" we had both shared as enthusiastic youngsters, up to when we went our different ways. He had been longing for a renewal and revival of the early enthusiastic faith and joy in the Holy Spirit, and as he read on, the warmth turned to heat.

Then, unexpectedly, he went to hear Michael Mitton of the Acorn Healing Trust preach, and in his talk, Michael mentioned his Glasshampton visits and our sharing contemplative prayer. Ron went up to him, made sure of my identity, and soon the letter arrived, full of warm reminiscences and longing for a fresh experience of the Holy Spirit.

We fixed a date, and Ron came to Glasshampton for the day. As soon as we met, though we were forty years different, the old fire was rekindled, the old fervor restored, and we were both filled with the Holy Spirit. The day was spent in Scripture, prayer, the sharing of experiences and eating a joyful meal together, until Ron went home in the evening.

Our exchange of letters since then has contained something of the sheer gratuitous joy of God's sustaining care over the years, and the stirring up of youth's energy, experience, and fire. When Ron wrote his first letter, he asked if I remembered him, and when I replied, I said, "Remember you, Ron? Why, I have just written a chapter in my mountain book on 'Mount Carmel,' and I quoted the hymn you taught me forty years ago":

> *God of Elijah, hear our cry:*
> *Send the fire!*
> *And make us fit to live or die:*
> *Send the fire!*
> *Oh, see us on Your altar lay*
> *Our lives, our all this very day;*
> *To crown the offering now, we pray:*
> *Send the fire!*

I shall send him this chapter for his approval later this week, and I can see his beaming face now as I recall our renewal of friendship.

The point I am making here is that as I prepared to write about Mary and Elizabeth, both filled with the Holy Spirit and leaping for joy, I immediately thought of Ron's coming to my hermitage and greeting me, and the "leaping for joy" we both experienced, though we cannot leap in quite as lively a way as we did when we were twenty years old.

The Holy Spirit in Elizabeth recognized the Holy Spirit in Mary. It is a matter of God recognizing God, and that was what Charles Wesley meant when he wrote:

> *The Spirit answers to the blood,*
> *And tells me I am born of God.*

It is also what John means when he writes, "Those who believe in the Son of God have the testimony in their hearts" (1 Jn 5:10), and what Paul means when he says, "When we cry, 'Abba! Father!' it is that very Spirit bearing witness with our spirit that we are children of God" (Rom 8:15–16).

Such leaping for joy is the consequence of the presence, blessing, and filling with the Holy Spirit. But it is also part of a wider story, a broader context, in the experience of Mary's pilgrimage and our own. Immense joy is communicated, but the same Spirit leads (and drives) us into the wilderness of pain and sorrow before the journey's done.

Prayer

Jesus, hidden in the womb of Mary: You dwell within the secret places of the heart, from whence you move us in compassion, stir us in enthusiasm, and kindle us in interior joy. You also dwell in the secret place of silence and pain, and we have to enter into our own depths to find out the meaning of your movement within. Give us joy when we meet others of like mind and experience, and prepare us for those times of difficulty and darkness that lie ahead—that at all times we may be faithful to your Spirit's leading.

Reflection

Value the experiences of sharing with a loved one, a friend, a fellow believer, and within the church fellowship in word and sacrament. Let such sharing be the source of joy and hope in our dark world, for the Spirit dwells secretly in the most unexpected places.

LENT 4: TUESDAY

Incarnation: God-Bearer

In those days a decree went out from Emperor Augustus that all the
world should be registered. This was the first registration and was
taken while Quirinius was governor of Syria. All went to their own
towns to be registered. Joseph also went from the town of Nazareth
in Galilee to Judea, to the city of David called Bethlehem, because
he was descended from the house and family of David. He went to
be registered with Mary, to whom he was engaged and who was
expecting a child. While they were there, the time came for her to
deliver her child. And she gave birth to her firstborn son and wrapped
him in bands of cloth, and laid him in a manger, because there was
no place for them in the inn.

LUKE 2:1–7

Elizabeth was old and barren, but she brought forth a new prophet
after four hundred years of silence; Zechariah was dumb, but he
sang a poetic canticle of redemption; now the time had come for the
promised virgin to give birth to the source of all light and life. Luke
has presented us with these three main characters in the drama of
Christ's Nativity. Now, as if for contrast, he presents Caesar Augustus.

Augustus reigned from 30 B.C. to A.D. 14 over an empire which
extended over the Mediterranean world eastward into Asia and west-
ward to the island of Britain. He represented wealth, power, and authority, was thought of as a god, and with the Pax Romana, the Roman
peace, was hailed as savior and prince of peace, and his edicts were
proclaimed as good news.

Into a tiny corner of this vast empire, one night a baby was born—
and his name was Jesus. Here are the two contrasting facts: Caesar
Augustus sent forth a decree (2:1); God sent forth his Son (Gal 4:4).

Augustus became an instrument in the hands of God as had Cyrus
of Persia before him (Isa 45:1), and his decree prepared the way for
the birth of the Messiah. The emperor's name is an echo in ancient
history, but the name of Jesus has been loved and revered through the

centuries since, and will one day be universally acknowledged as Savior, Lord, and Prince of Peace, before whom every knee shall joyfully and humbly bow (Phil 2:10–11).

We are remembering the motherhood of Mary and the nativity of Jesus during our Lenten journey because there is an intimate human connection between birth and death, and the incarnation of Jesus as an infant plants his small feet on the road that leads to the cross.

The image of Madonna and Child is a universal, archetypal symbol for the Christian and non-Christian alike, and it reaches deep into the human psyche of birth and death. In my hermitage chapel I have a version of the famous icon "Our Lady of Vladimir." The original was painted in Constantinople about A.D. 1130, and went to Russia as part of the Orthodox Faith. It is the most famous of the *Theotokos* icons. *Theotokos* means "God-bearer." If this proper translation had been made from the Greek of the Council of Ephesus in A.D. 431, instead of going through the Latin *Mater Dei* and translated Mother of God, a lot of misunderstanding would have been avoided.

The term was coined to affirm the divinity of Christ, not to glorify Mary, or if glory is to be rightly given to Mary it is because of her Son and Savior. In this sense evangelical Christians could use the term "Mother of God" not to imply that Mary is the mother of the Trinity, but as the mother of Jesus in whom God became incarnate. She is therefore *Theotokos*, God-bearer.

My version of the icon is that painted by Brother Eric of the Taizé community. It communicates the profound tenderness of the original—the maternal, compassionate, and sorrowing Mary, and the vulnerable, dependent affection of the infant. And already, in the halo around the infant's head, there is the form of a cross.

These birth narratives of Matthew and Luke are not found in the other gospels, and they providentially preserve an early tradition in the Church. (Readers wanting to examine the scholarly aspects of the birth narratives will find all they need in the exhaustive work of Raymond E. Brown, *The Birth of the Messiah*, Doubleday, 1993.) In both Matthew and Luke the narratives lead on from the joy and wonder brought to birth with the Christ Child in Mary's heart, to the sorrow of following his life and ministry into risk and danger, the "let-ting-go" into the deepening will of God, and at last to the foot of the cross.

It even begins in these first few verses where we are told that there was no place for them in the inn, foreshadowing the rejection of Jesus by his own people (Jn 1:11). But just now, the simple poverty of the scene depicts the joy and treasure in Mary's heart, and we would do well to rejoice with her before we move on—for move we must.

Prayer

No room for the baby at Bethlehem's inn,
　Only a cattle shed;
No room on this earth for the dear Son of God,
　Nowhere to lay his head;
Only a cross did they give to my Lord,
　Only a borrowed tomb;
Just now he is waiting a place in my heart,
　Shall I still say to him, "No room!"?

Reflection

Already here there is a parting of the ways; those who come to the manger to kneel, and those who thrust the Christ aside with the words "No room!" It was not out of hostility that the pregnant Mary was refused, but because of a crowd of other people, other matters. Indif-ference to the child she bore was due to a lack of recognition that in her, and in her Son, the divine love is offered to the human heart. We may say "no room" to the gospel message, or to the unmarried mother of our own day—both come to the same thing in the end, for "just as you did it to one of the least of these who are members of my family, you did it to me" (Mt 25:40).

—✠—

LENT 4: WEDNESDAY

Presentation:
A Sword Will Pierce Your Soul

Now there was a man in Jerusalem whose name was Simeon; this man was righteous and devout, looking forward to the consolation of Israel, and the Holy Spirit rested on him. It had been revealed to him by the Holy Spirit that he would not see death before he had seen the Lord's Messiah. Guided by the Spirit, Simeon came into the temple; and when the parents brought in the child Jesus, to do for him what was customary under the law, Simeon took him in his arms and praised God, saying, "Master, now you are dismissing your servant in peace, according to your word; for my eyes have seen your salvation, which you have prepared in the presence of all peoples, a light for revelation to the Gentiles and for glory to your people Israel." And the child's father and mother were amazed at what was being said about him. Then Simeon blessed them and said to his mother Mary, "This child is destined for the falling and rising of many in Israel, and to be a sign that will be opposed so that the inner thoughts of many will be revealed—and a sword will pierce your own soul too."

LUKE 2:25–35

The whole scene shifts now from Bethlehem to Jerusalem. We have spoken of the Ark of the Covenant coming to Jerusalem, and of Mary's medieval title "the Ark of God" which is overshadowed by the presence and glory of God. The Ark had long since been lost (Jer 3:16), and the Holy of Holies within the inner veil of the temple was now empty. Now, as prophesied by Malachi (3:1–4), the Lord comes to his temple for reasons of glory and purification—for mercy and for judgment, and these are the notes which are struck in today's passage.

Doubtless there were other parents bringing their children with the prescribed offerings, and Jesus, along with them, was received, but unrecognized by the official priesthood in the temple. But sud-

denly, old Simeon appears, guided by the Holy Spirit and with a charismatic authority which allows him to take Jesus into his arms, and
break forth into the beautiful song we call the *Nunc Dimittis*, leading
to a prophecy of glory and sorrow for the child, for Mary, for Israel
and for the whole Gentile world.

This Feast of the Presentation is also called Candlemas, and here
in Glasshampton monastery we process along the cloister to the chapel,
with lit candles in our hands, singing the *Nunc Dimittis*, and praising
Christ the light, who pierces the darkness of our world. The next time
we shall process with candles will be at the Easter Vigil, when we
move from the sorrows of the death of Jesus into his radiant rising on
Easter Day. But there is much grief between.

Luke says that Mary and Joseph were amazed at Simeon's prophecy, and it is here we must pause to ask what it is that Mary now
understands, from the annunciation by Gabriel up to this moment.
First, she has learned that this mysterious child of hers is the Davidic
Messiah come to redeem his people from their sins, and to usher in
the kingdom of righteousness and peace. Then the circle widens, for
he is not only Israel's light, but a light to the whole Gentile world. At
the moment of Simeon's prophecy the temple becomes a house of
prayer for all people (Isa 56:7; Mk 11:17).

Then comes the warning of suffering. Sorrow's sword shall pierce
the heart of Mary because her dear Son will suffer in the work of
redemption. The path, from wonder through suffering to glory, makes
the full circle, and Mary enters even more deeply into the price and
pain of her motherhood.

Simeon can weep as he sings, for it is a double-edged message,
but for him there is the precious experience of fulfillment of the promise which the Spirit has made that he would not die until he had seen
the Lord's Messiah. And close upon his prophecy, the eighty-four-
year-old Anna appeared, who had spent decades of contemplative
prayer in the temple, and she closes the scene with praise and proclamation of the child who was to become the Messiah-Redeemer.

We are present at this scene, and we participate in both its joy and
sorrow, entering into the promise and amazement which marked the

group gathered around the Christ Child. The fourteenth-century Franciscan saint Angela of Foligno speaks of a vision she had on this feast, when she saw Mary enter the temple, and she followed with great reverence and godly fear. This is how she continues:

> Our Lady herself gave my soul great security, and held out to me her Son Jesus, and said: "O lover of my Son, take him!" and she placed her Son in my arms, and he seemed to me to have his eyes closed as if he slept, and he was wrapped in swaddling clothes. Moreover, Our Lady sat down as if wearied by her journey, and made such beautiful and pleasing signs, and her presence was so good and gracious, and it was so sweet and pleasant a thing to see her, that my soul not only regarded the Child Jesus, whom she held so closely in her arms, but was forced also to look upon his mother.... And the look in the Child's eyes made me feel such love that I was overcome. For from those eyes there went forth so great a splendor and fire of love and joy, that it is unutterable.

> *IN ELIZABETH RUTH OBBARD, A YEAR WITH MARY,*
> *(THE CANTERBURY PRESS: 1998)*

Prayer

Jesus, held in Simeon's arms: Enable me to take you in my arms, to hold you in my heart, to allow your light to irradiate my being. Show me, Jesus, the path of joy and suffering, and prepare me to walk closely in the way that Mary trod, that after the pain and sorrow I may also with her enter into joy.

Reflection

Both Simeon and Anna, like Elizabeth and Zechariah, belonged to the "anawim," the poor people who looked for a Messiah, not of violence and political power, but of peace, light, and joy. Will you allow this vision of the Christ to possess your imagination, and influence your way of living and relating to all around you at all levels of your life?

LENT 4: THURSDAY

Contemplation: Treasure in Her Heart

Now every year [Jesus'] parents went to Jerusalem for the festival of the Passover. And when he was twelve years old, they went up as usual for the festival. When the festival was ended and they started to return, the boy Jesus stayed behind in Jerusalem, but his parents did not know it. Assuming that he was in the group of travelers, they went a day's journey. Then they started to look for him among their relatives and friends. When they did not find him, they returned to Jerusalem to search for him. After three days they found him in the temple, sitting among the teachers, listening to them and asking them questions. And all who heard him were amazed at his understanding and his answers. When his parents saw him they were astonished; and his mother said to him, "Child, why have you treated us like this? Look, your father and I have been searching for you in great anxiety." He said to them, "Why were you searching for me? Did you not know that I must be in my Father's house?" But they did not understand what he said to them. Then he went down with them and came to Nazareth, and was obedient to them. His mother treasured all these things in her heart.

LUKE 2:41–51

T his is a precious passage from the hidden years of Jesus, and re-corded only in Luke. The early Church was not concerned to record incidents from Jesus' childhood, though later there emerged a collection of apocryphal gospels with all kinds of precocious and startling wonders which were wisely kept out of the New Testament canon. This story is all the more precious for its rarity and its restraint in presentation.

Luke likes recording journeys, and as we are looking through Mary's eyes this week, we see that this is the third journey in which she enters more deeply into the mystical and spiritual understanding of Jesus' greater pilgrimage.

First of all there was the journey to Ain Karim, after the Annunciation, where she and Elizabeth experienced the leaping for joy and inward testimony of the Holy Spirit. Then there was the journey to Bethlehem where, as a result of the birth and the shepherd's story, Mary "treasured all these words and pondered them in her heart." And in today's passage we have recorded the journey to Jerusalem where, after perplexity, searching, and astonishment, Luke records, "His mother treasured all these things in her heart."

So quite apart from the years of preparation, of which we know nothing, Mary has been overshadowed, indwelt, and filled by the Spirit of contemplation. The words *pondering* and *treasuring* speak of gathering together carefully, guarding, meditating, and holding her inward thoughts in and before the Spirit of God.

It was when Jesus was twelve years old that Mary and Joseph took him to the Passover festival at Jerusalem—what would become later, for a Jewish boy, his bar mitzvah (child of the law). The seven-day festival ended, and the travelers from Mary's village started off back to Nazareth—about eighty miles, assuming Jesus was in the company. After a day's journey they realized that he was missing, and returned to Jerusalem with great anxiety to search for him.

They eventually came to the outer courts of the temple where the teachers and scribes were involved in theological and spiritual discussion. There was Jesus listening, questioning, and answering; provoking amazement among the doctors of the law. Luke does not portray him as theologically precocious, but possessing an open and lively mind, curious in his questions and intuitive in his responses.

When Mary and Joseph intervene, speaking of their concern and anxiety, Jesus amazes them by saying that he must be in his Father's house. Mary had said, "Your father and I..." and Jesus had responded with "my Father's house." Luke is making it clear that Jesus' origins and concerns transcend his human family. As Jesus would later maintain, "My mother and my brothers are those who hear the word of God and do it" (8:21).

For Jesus to speak of "my Father" and "my Father's house" was startling both to the teachers and to his parents. Here is the unique relationship to the Father that Jesus was affirming intuitively at twelve years of age, together with the divine necessity (verse 49) of doing just what they found him doing—pursuing the will of his Father.

Although Mary and Joseph did not understand at that point, he obeyed, and returned with them. But Mary was already pondering, meditating, even treasuring these things. Here was a long-distance warning, and she was already realizing that she had to let go, and yet follow him in heart and mind.

In our own lives we must first of all make sure that Jesus is among us, in the company. If he is not, then we must pursue our search, seek him with all our hearts, find him in the "temple" which represents the overshadowing of the Holy Spirit, the place where Scripture is read and prayer is offered.

When we have found him, then he is to be enthroned in the temple of our hearts, and we should follow that up by treasuring his words, his will and his leading as the pattern of our own lives.

Prayer

Jesus in the temple: Bestow upon us open minds, curious searching and responsive hearts; enable us to understand the divine necessity which took you to your Father's house, and caused your mother Mary to ponder more deeply the beginning of your pilgrimage and ministry. Then enable us to make our own journey of faith and love, with a more contemplative and more dedicated will.

Reflection

Luke makes this episode a link between the birth narratives and the baptism and ministry of Jesus. The story moves on, and we must move on with it. Mary had inward contemplative resources for her letting go and moving on. So, too, for us, the resources unfolding in our interior life provide insight and strength for our journey.

— ✠ —

LENT 4: FRIDAY

Celebration: Do Whatever He Tells You

On the third day there was a wedding in Cana of Galilee, and the mother of Jesus was there. Jesus and his disciples had also been invited to the wedding. When the wine gave out, the mother of Jesus said to him, "They have no wine." And Jesus said to her, "Woman, what concern is that to you and to me? My hour has not yet come." His mother said to the servants, "Do whatever he tells you." Now standing there were six stone water jars for the Jewish rites of purification, each holding twenty or thirty gallons. Jesus said to them, "Fill the jars with water." And they filled them up to the brim. He said to them, "Now draw some out, and take it to the chief steward." So they took it. When the steward tasted the water that had become wine, and did not know where it came from (though the servants who had drawn the water knew), the steward called the bridegroom and said to him, "Everyone serves the good wine first, and then the inferior wine after the guests have become drunk. But you have kept the good wine until now." Jesus did this, the first of his signs, in Cana of Galilee, and revealed his glory; and his disciples believed in him.

JOHN 2:1–11

Mary is at the center of today's celebration. But then she points to the true center—Christ the bringer of wine and the heavenly bridegroom. We tend to associate Mary with simple purity, trusting obedience, and profound sorrow. These things are true, but we must not miss the note of celebration which is being struck today.

We find her midway between the infancy and childhood narratives of Jesus and his launching out into his risky and amazing public ministry by today's manifestation of glory in his first sign. There is a Coptic tradition that Mary is a relative of the bride's mother, and she does seem to have some authority in the story. We see her here taking the initiative, bearing something of the responsibility, and turning to Jesus for his solution to the dilemma of wine running out—which would be a cause of real shame for the wedding hosts.

This outward, joyful, celebratory life of Mary is simply the over-flowing of her rich interior life. All through the years, hidden in her heart, the revelation of who Jesus was has been the subject of her thoughts, dreams, fears, and hopes. She has spent many hours in the quietness of the working days, thinking about who Jesus really was. She has watched him in his daily life, his hours of prayer in the hills above Nazareth, and she has spent many waking hours of the night in meditation and prayer.

Therefore, today's celebration is that aspect of her life in which there is joy, gladness, and inebriation—the source of which is not the wine, but Christ himself, for she certainly embodied the joy contained in the words: "Do not get drunk with wine...but be filled with the Spirit, as you sing psalms and hymns and spiritual songs...singing and making melody to the Lord in your hearts, giving thanks to God the Father at all times and for everything in the name of our Lord Jesus Christ" (Eph 5:18–20).

When Mary got word of the shortage of wine from the master of ceremonies of the feast, she immediately turned to Jesus, and though the Greek text is not as abrupt as the English translation appears, Jesus does seem to be indicating that he is not simply a wonder-worker. All that he does is in the light of "his hour" of destiny, and this is the whole purpose for which he was born, the hour of his glory, when he would be lifted up from the earth and draw all people to himself.

Everything he did, therefore, had this aim and motive in mind, and in his response to Mary he was reminding her of this very thing. The sign of transforming water into wine was the first manifestation of the glory which would culminate in the return to the glory which he shared with the Father before the world was made (17:5).

Such high theology, in John's hand, is spelled out in this simple, joyful domestic scene in which Jesus comes to the rescue, and at the same time reveals his glory in saving the bride and groom from shame and loss of face. Mary understands all this. She has been meditating upon it long enough, and turning to the servants she says, "Do what-ever he tells you."

What blessing flows from these words. The servants obey Jesus in filling the six cleansing waterpots to the brim with water, then carrying wine to the steward who exploded with pleasure at the quality and the effect that this new wine had upon him—an inebriating experience of joy. Only a few people were in on the secret of Jesus' transforming power—and Mary's faith was at the heart of the secret.

The amount of wine was absurd—between 120 and 180 gallons of the stuff. This reminds me of a gospel song I used to sing as a boy:

> *Grace flowing like a river,*
> *Millions there have been supplied;*
> *Still it flows as fresh as ever*
> *From the Savior's wounded side.*

Wine is the symbol of the blood of the new covenant with its cleansing, renewing, and inebriating power. And the real miracle of this sign at Cana was the transformation of the disciples by the creative love of Jesus manifesting his glory.

Can you feel the simple joy that filled Mary's heart as the look of awareness and gratitude passed between them when she and Jesus shared a cup of wine together? This was a moment of celebration, and one which would sustain her as now Jesus prepares to embark on a series of signs of glory which would bring forgiveness, healing, and good news to the common people, but which would also bring down on his head the suspicion, hatred, and evil plotting of the authorities.

Jesus was a man of true joy, creativity, and transformation—and such men are often hated by those whose lives are narrow, bigoted, and embittered, in forms of power and religion that shrivel their hearts and ultimately condemn their souls to darkness.

Our celebration of the Savior's transforming power must issue in good, healthy, hopeful, and joyful lives. This will manifest the glory of Christ in the world which desperately needs him. But it must be followed by heeding the words which Mary spoke from the wisdom of her own experience, "Do whatever he tells you."

Prayer

Jesus, Master of the feast: You are the bringer of new wine, the provider of joy and gladness. Melancholy and despair have no part in your saving gospel, so forgive your people for taking their eyes from you and living in the valley of depression and fear. Lift our eyes and hearts to glimpse your glory, as Mary did, and fill our lives with inebriating joy.

Reflection

Does your life reflect the joy of Jesus' transforming love, and would your neighbors think of you as a person of humor and joy? This joy does not mean levity, false optimism, or a secular pursuit of happiness—that's a transient dream. Gospel joy is based upon obedience to the will of God, and that embraces pain and suffering along the way. Get these things in perspective as Mary did, and let your joy be the overflow and consequence of abiding in the will of God.

— ✝ —

LENT 4: SATURDAY

Crucifixion: Here Is Your Mother

Standing near the cross of Jesus were his mother, and his mother's sister, Mary the wife of Clopas, and Mary Magdalene. When Jesus saw his mother and the disciple whom he loved standing beside her, he said to his mother, "Woman, here is your son." Then he said to the disciple, "Here is your mother." And from that hour the disciple took her into his own home.

JOHN 19:25–27

If there is anyone of whom it can be asked, "Were you there?" it is Mary, the mother of Jesus. She was there in immense sadness and pain as Jesus hung upon the cross; and she was there continually in the days following, full of heartfelt joy as the light which streamed from the cross filled her soul before the risen Christ. But before the joy came the sorrow.

We have been here before, when we stood at the foot of the cross with the beloved disciple. But now we see it through the eyes of Mary. And for Mary the crucifixion is anchored within the Incarnation. It is physical, bodily, fleshly suffering, and for us human beings, so much of our pain and glory is rooted in the body.

Yet here, at the foot of the cross, though my pity and pain is not maternal suffering, yet I do weep, because I have wept at the pain and dying of others, and I have been at the bedside of many dying people, and felt their mortality and finitude—reflecting on my own.

It is a wonderful thing to be human, to be embodied, to feel the warmth and affection of another's embrace, the linking of hands, the recognition of a smile, the simple, basic, physical things we share with one another. As one grows from early youth into manhood and womanhood, there are all the creative joys of walking, meditative awareness on a beautiful autumn day, the use of arms, hands, and fingers in music-making, drawing, painting, and the totality of limbs and body in various sports—and love-making.

There are physical recompenses, too, as the years go by, for if others' experience is anything like my own, with the funny sadness of lost abilities (I cannot cycle from Swansea to Cardigan on a Friday evening as I used to), there are the increasingly deeper catchings of breath in a more profound insight into color, light, harmony, texture, taste—and contemplative relaxation. The popular song can be interpreted at many levels: "Love is lovelier the second time around…."

Mary was embodied—and felt it acutely in all parts of her body and heart that related to her beloved Son. She stands today at the foot of the cross, and we shall stand with her throughout Holy Week as we hear and meditate upon the seven words from the cross.

There is one more picture which follows on from today's Scripture, and it is portrayed in marble loveliness in Michelangelo's *Pietà*, in Saint Peter's, Rome. Mary holds the embodied Jesus in her arms after he has been taken down from the cross. In all the body language of that masterly sculpture, there is utter stillness, beautiful passivity, and the strange, faithful waiting…before the darkness of Calvary is pierced by the light of hope and glory.

Prayer

Jesus, carried in the womb of Mary: You were bonded to Mary your mother by the ties of our physical humanity, of her flesh and her bone, and thus made one with us. Give us joy in our bodily lives, that our bodies may become worthy temples of the Holy Spirit, and our invigorated flesh become the instrument of enlightened spirit.

Reflection

Have you stood, sat or knelt in sorrow with others? Have you shared in the pain or dying of a loved one, and reached out hand and heart in tears and feeling of fellowship? Have you been touched, held, embraced, by another's love or pain? Count all these as precious, and reach out physically today—to help, uplift, link, or celebrate the embodiment of your physical and spiritual life. For we are rooted and grounded in the body.

Lent 5

—✠—

Drawn to the Cross

LENT 5: SUNDAY

Mary Magdalene:
Lenten Darkness, Easter Hope

[Jesus] went on through cities and villages, proclaiming and bringing the good news of the kingdom of God. The twelve were with
him, as well as some women....Mary, called Magdalene, from whom
seven demons had gone out....

LUKE 8:1–3

Joseph took the body...and laid it in his own new tomb, which he
had hewn in the rock. He then rolled a great stone to the door of the
tomb and went away. Mary Magdalene and the other Mary were
there, sitting opposite the tomb....

MATTHEW 27:59–61

Early on the first day of the week, while it was still dark, Mary
Magdalene came to the tomb and saw that the stone had been
removed....So she ran and went to Simon Peter and the other disciples, the one whom Jesus loved, and said to them, "They have
taken the Lord out of the tomb, and we do not know where they
have laid him."

JOHN 20:1–2

Mary Magdalene is the center of our attention today. There is much
that can be said about her, but in our Lenten journey there are
three words which we need to take to our own hearts, illustrated in her
life. They are: *conversion, waiting, recognizing.* Let's look at them:

Conversion. Traditionally, Mary Magdalene is the prostitute exor-
cized and converted from her life of shame and sin, and that is the
Magdalene we find in Jesus Christ, Superstar, singing, "I don't know
how to love him...." But we really do not know the nature of the "seven
devils" and it may well have been a serious mental disorder from which
Jesus delivered her. Certainly she had experienced a deliverance and

conversion, and could have sung with profound feeling, "ransomed, healed, restored, forgiven…" by the grace of Christ. As a result of her conversion, she gave up her home, and joined with the band of women who accompanied Jesus and the Twelve, ministering to them as they ministered to the people in preaching and healing. All these women seemed to have undergone profound conversion experiences, and they were a holy band who don't have much press in the gospels, but they are there, with an undergirding ministry of sustenance and prayer.

Waiting. In our second passage of Scripture we have Mary waiting. Here she is waiting at the tomb, but earlier in the chapter she is waiting at the foot of the cross. The active ministry is often easier than the passive one. "They also serve who only stand and wait," but it is not something many of us relish, for there is a certain helplessness about it, and the climate of our times is completely against it. It is when we have no resources, financial, physical, or mental that we have to wait— perhaps when we are ill, waiting to be seen, waiting for surgery, waiting for appointments or therapy, among others who are also waiting. Or waiting at the bedside of loved ones, waiting for a broken relationship to be repaired, waiting for a lost one to return to your heart's love…waiting. After the waiting at the foot of the cross, Mary followed to the rock-hewn tomb, and waited there. The time of waiting was not wasted, for unless we wait upon the Lord our strength will never be renewed, and unless we wait in patient hope, the dawn of the sun's rising will never come.

Recognizing. This is a somewhat premature word for Lent, but we can speak the word as a foretaste of what we hope for as a word of faith. We have to take the word at its basic, etymological meaning— recognize—to see again that which we had looked upon earlier; to experience again that which was once precious and life-giving; to think through again those early bright promises of faith and hope which have become dimmed by disappointment, compromise, and long wearisome waiting.

It is a result of waiting, at the cross and the tomb, that Mary was able to be in the right place at the right time. She lived through her

Lent, and strangely, suddenly, dramatically, entered into her Easter. And she was the one who witnessed and experienced the risen Christ, and proclaimed the astounding news to the fearful and depressed disciples. But we are not there yet, and we must learn to walk the way of sorrow, of waiting, of Calvary, before we can enter into glory.

These three words should mark every Lenten pilgrim. Unless there is experience of conversion, we cannot really begin the journey, for conversion is the beginning. I don't mean a flash conversion which has no abiding power or rootedness. But I do mean a true turning to God—in a moment or as a process—and a daily conversion of the heart from all that is not love, towards the One who by his cross and passion has redeemed us.

Then we must learn the patience of waiting—in discipleship, in contemplative prayer, in patient serving of our sisters and brothers in love. And not least, the daily waiting upon ourselves in patience, allowing the experience of our lives, both positive and negative, to mellow and mature us, and make us more human and more compassionate.

If these two things are in place—conversion and waiting—then we shall enter ever more deeply into a recognition and discernment of the spiritual life. We shall learn to live through our darkness and the world's darkness without fear—for there is the promise of the dawn of light and glory on ahead. Dark night always gives way to dawn; Lent always gives way to Easter; Mary Magdalene's loving, patient perplexity at the empty tomb in the morning led her ultimately to behold the Sun of Righteousness in all his glory.

Prayer

Jesus, patient Redeemer: Mary Magdalene's conversion experience was only the beginning of her journey of discipleship, and her growth in grace was the result of patient waiting at the foot of the cross and the empty tomb. Grant me true conversion, so that my feet may be firmly set upon the way, then continue your work in giving me patience in prayer, in service, in compassion. Then shall the Easter dawn begin to shed its light upon my path, leading me at last to the glory which is beyond the present darkness.

Reflection

*Are these three words—*conversion, waiting, *and* recognition—*indicative of your own spiritual life and that of the church community with whom you meet in word and sacrament? It is possible to substitute human effort for true conversion, to substitute frenetic activity for patient waiting in prayer, and to try to bring in the kingdom of God by political manipulation. We need to give heart, mind, and hand to personal and social concerns—but only from the creative source of a truly converted life.*

—— ✠ ——

LENT 5: MONDAY

Simon: Carrying His Cross

They compelled a passer-by, who was coming in from the country, to carry his cross; it was Simon of Cyrene, the father of Alexander and Rufus. Then they brought Jesus to the place called Golgotha (which means the place of the skull)....

MARK 15:21–22

Greet Rufus, chosen in the Lord; and greet his mother—a mother to me also.

ROMANS 16:13

Today's journey is on the *via dolorosa*, the way of sorrows, where Jesus is led out of the Praetorium where the soldiers had mocked him in the purple robe, crown of thorns, and reed scepter. They did not know what they were doing, yet these were strange symbols of regal power and majesty.

The cruel flogging with a long lash, studded with sharpened pieces of bone and lead pellets left the body with raw flesh and bleeding welts. Men had gone mad or died under it. Jesus suffered by such scourging and was mocked by soldiers through the night, and then was thrust forth, bearing the crossbeam on which he would be crucified.

It was at this point that Simon was drawn to the cross. He was from distant Cyrene in North Africa, perhaps fulfilling a life's ambition in coming to Jerusalem for the Passover. And now he was conscripted by a soldier to this dreadful task.

We speak of "taking up the cross of Jesus," but in our ears it frequently means a way of following, with a dash of asceticism, a few luxuries given up, or a tithe of income we can well afford. If the cross in all its stark nakedness and fierce demand was shown to us, we should run away, change our mind, reconsider. The strange thing is that Simon was "drawn" to the *via dolorosa*—and what happened was not what he intended.

So it is with us. We are drawn to the beauty and loveliness of the cross of forgiveness, with its light and joy piercing the darkness of our sin and perplexity. And then, when we begin to savor its genuine beauty, we begin to see that there is another dimension to bearing the cross. We are, as it were, conscripted, compelled, to go on. There seems no alternative, and when we take up the crossbeam in fear and trepidation, we find that we are actually lifting the burden, or at least sharing it, with our Lord.

Can you imagine the horror with which Simon accepted the crossbeam taken from the exhausted Jesus, and laid roughly on his shoulders by a soldier? Can you see the gratitude he glimpsed in the eyes of Jesus, through the sweat and blood of his forehead and face? Can you begin to imagine the awful realization of where his journey was going to end—for Jesus and for Simon?

Should he have rebelled, refused, tried to intercede, for the poor prisoner whose hands and feet were to be nailed, whose body would be transfixed between heaven and earth? I think, perhaps, Simon would have been able to sing that old passion hymn with profound emotion in later Easter days:

> *Upon that cross of Jesus*
> *My eye at times can see*
> *The very dying form of One*
> *Who suffered there for me.*
> *And from my stricken heart, with tears,*
> *Two wonders I confess—*
> *The wonders of his glorious love,*
> *And my unworthiness.*

And so it is with us. There comes a time when the sweetness ends and the darkness begins. There is no other way, for we must tread the long Lenten path before the glory of Easter dawns. No Lent, no Easter.

This is the meaning behind the dedication of this book to Pauline and Tim. Pauline was one of the old Anglican deaconesses, and we had a correspondence over the years, with immense joy. She was a valiant Christian, and when she heard that I had been ill, she wrote with perceptive understanding, and told me that she was "on her last lap" in her eighties, in a Bristol nursing home. She also told me that there was one thing she wanted me to do for her. Would I pray for, and write to, Tim, a young man who was suffering from a form of cancer which seemed terminal?

So I prayed and wrote. Tim and I began a correspondence which lasted during the last three months of his life, as he moved towards his own death. What joy we had in sharing, in praying, in trusting for healing or for a good and gentle death. At one point I had two separate letters from both Pauline and Tim, telling me of the same conversation they shared, centering around a passage in my book, *A Hidden Fire*, in which I had expounded the apostle Paul's words in 2 Timothy 4:6–7: "I am already being poured out as a libation, and the time of my departure has come. I have fought the good fight, I have finished the race, I have kept the faith...."

Tim told me that he and Pauline had both counted on being "called home" soon. Having been a Christian for only a short while, he felt it was now time to be baptized—and he indicated that it was a preparation for his death. None of this was dark or negative. Indeed, there was a spirit of acceptance, not resignation, in Tim's attitude, and I was very moved by it.

The next thing that happened was that when Pauline realized that the connection between Tim and myself had been made, and that all things were in place, she closed her eyes and died. Tim and I both affirmed the meaning in that.

Tim went with his mother and brother for a break to the Philippines, and I received a card from him which is before me now—with Mount Apo, the highest peak rising from green lowlands, through a ring of white cloud. He wrote: "Ramon, I continue to cherish you in my prayers...." and I held him up to the heart of God as I read those words.

Only a few days later, I had a letter from Tim's parents, who just returned from the Philippines, telling me that their dear son, Tim, had died in the early hours of the previous Tuesday morning.

His letter to me, of a month previously, shared his love of life, family, and of all the things he wanted to do and the awareness of the path that had led him, through reflection and pain, to place everything in God's hands and accept the outcome. It is a letter of such maturity and beauty, and of immense gratitude to Pauline for bringing us together. With powerful realism, in the midst of his suffering, he continued: "I have certainly grown spiritually as a result of this experience. Ultimately I just rest in the assurance of God's eternal love for me, and the knowledge that through the saving power of Christ's blood shed on the cross, I need not fear death whenever it may come." And it came a month later—to the very day.

He and Pauline traversed their Lenten path with pain and joy, in darkness and in light. None of their words were spoken lightly, for their suffering was different, but real. Yet on that dark Lent path the light of future glory was already shining, and the radiance of their departure shines on in their family, their church community, and in my heart.

God did not send their illness and cancer, but like Simon of Cyrene, the cross was imposed upon them, and when they had received it with all its grief and burden, the Lord turned its darkness into light, and it continues to be a means of grace and glory—yet not without tears—which well up within me as I write, and which I know will be reciprocated when John and Di, Tim's parents, read these lines.

In the case of Simon of Cyrene, too, the story goes on. For Mark tells us that he was the father of Alexander and Rufus (15:21), so he must have known them as believers when he wrote his Gospel. Then we meet Rufus in Paul's letter to the Romans: "Greet Rufus, chosen in the Lord; and greet his mother—a mother to me also" (16:13). Then again in Acts 13:1 there is a list of godly men among whom is named Simeon (Simon) called Niger—the usual name at that time for a man of dark skin from Africa.

From that episode of pain and darkness on the Calvary road, Simon is touched, moved, and converted to the love of Christ—and the joy keeps on multiplying and the glory keeps on spreading.

Prayer

Jesus, bearer of the cross: You call me to take up the cross of light and forgiveness, and this I do with eager longing. You call me to take up the cross of suffering, persecution, and devoted service, and I hesitate, and look into your eyes of compassion. I hear your call; give me the strength to respond with joy.

Reflection

I wrote the following words in response to Tim's valiant letter. Can you receive them for yourself?

> *The Lord blesses, heals, forgives, and holds us close to himself simply because he loves us. That means that if we were too tired, ill, or weary to give much time or effort even to prayer, we only have to rest and fall into his love, and ultimately he will carry us through...it is enough that you are there and I am here, and the link of love and prayer is there for us both. I believe that Pauline's dying act was to link us together, and that was the Lord's gift, too. I don't know how much believers in the dimension of eternity are allowed to know about us, but I believe the Lord communicates words of love to them more directly than is possible for us in our present state. And if that is so, Pauline "knows" of our links, prays for us, and rejoices.*

— ✝ —

LENT 5: TUESDAY

Centurion: Confession of Faith

Then Jesus cried again with a loud voice and breathed his last. At
that moment the curtain of the temple was torn in two, from top to
bottom. The earth shook, and the rocks were split. The tombs also
were opened, and many bodies of the saints who had fallen asleep
were raised....Now when the centurion and those with him, who
were keeping watch over Jesus, saw the earthquake and what took
place, they were terrified and said, "Truly this man was God's Son!"

MATTHEW 27:50–54

I have just stepped out of my makeshift living quarters into the
cold and misty morning darkness, and into my chapel to light the
votive light and look on the person of the centurion portrayed on the
left of the crucified Jesus in my large Franciscan icon of the crucifixion. His face is filled with wonder; his eyes are fixed on the crucified Jesus; his right hand's fingers form a blessing and he has some
kind of parchment in his left hand. All this grows out of the three
Synoptic accounts of the interior response of this Roman soldier to
Jesus crucified and the surrounding events.

We shall concentrate on the response of the centurion, but it is
important to note that Matthew calls attention to what happened when
Jesus "gave up his spirit" as the Greek text says, indicating that even
in that last moment, perhaps especially then, Jesus voluntarily laid
down his life (see also Jn 10:17–18).

First, the veil of the temple guarding the Holy of Holies was torn
from top to bottom. There are two elements here—of judgment and
mercy. The first is a judgment of God upon all religious institutions
which crucify the Son of God. The apocryphal Gospel to the He-
brews says that the whole lintel holding the veil collapsed and was
shattered. This judgment was the divine comment upon the whole
religious system that crucifies love and identifies itself with power,
status, and control.

There is also (and this is primary) the gracious mercy that proclaims that there is now no more veil barring the way. All people are invited into the divine presence through the death of Jesus, for all divisions have now been removed. In Christ, the faraway God has come near, we are drawn into the divine presence, and the division between priest and believer, Jew and Gentile, bond and free, is abolished—for all who will avail themselves of it.

Then comes a strange story that only Matthew records. There is a cosmic response to the death of Jesus. As well as the darkness that veiled the face of the sun (verse 45), the earth shook and the rocks were split. This Scripture is reflected in the Franciscan story that the mountain La Verna on which Saint Francis received the stigmata in 1224 was also split at the moment when Jesus gave up his spirit. The accompanying words in our passage tell us of tombs being opened and holy ones rising and appearing to people in Jerusalem to accompany the resurrection of Jesus. This is nowhere else reported, but whatever else it means, it witnesses that Jesus conquered the grave, and that death has lost its ultimate power and terror, for Jesus is the "first fruits of those who have died" (1 Cor 15:20).

Now the centurion. The New Testament depicts centurions as worthy men, unlike their tyrannical and dissolute masters such as Herod or Pilate. The Capernaum centurion had a good reputation among the Jews (Mt 8:5), and the centurion Cornelius honored God in prayer and righteousness (Acts 10:1). Our centurion has been called Longinus or Petronius with tales woven around him, and he witnessed the last three hours with increasing wonder and awe. It became clear to him that Jesus who acted in life and death with dignity, calm, courage, and fortitude, was not a criminal or a man of treason, in contrast to the cursing thieves. Luke has him praising God and saying, "Certainly this man was innocent" (23:47).

In Matthew and Mark, he makes some kind of confession, "Truly this man was God's Son!" He may have meant a kind of Greco-Roman demigod according to his lights, but the Gospel writers certainly intend this confession to imply the recognition of divinity. He had experienced the strange cosmic events, and as the centurion in charge of the execution had possibly witnessed the conversion of the repentant thief, and the whole attitude of the dying Jesus. Together with some of the other soldiers, his soldier's watch become a disciple's vigil, and he became some kind of believer. He was certainly included in Jesus' prayer, "Father, forgive them…" (Lk 23:34), and was surely among those "other sheep" that Jesus included in his flock (Jn 10:16).

Prayer

Jesus, dying in courage and fortitude: I am there, Lord, with the centurion, the soldiers and the witnesses; I have my part in the responsibility for your passion and death. Give me a sense of wonder and awe, a spirit of true repentance, and the courage to confess you before others. Grant me a calm assurance in my life, and a good and gentle death at the last.

Reflection

The centurion was arrested by the whole episode of Calvary, and allowed his rough and toughened soldier's heart to be touched and moved by this dying man. Is your heart less touched, your spirit less awed, your will less moved, by the dying Savior? In these times of Lenten reflection, simply let your mind be open to all that God would accomplish, so that in you the promise may be fulfilled, "And I, when I am lifted up from the earth, will draw all people to myself" (Jn 12:32).

LENT 5: WEDNESDAY

Penitent Thief: Remember Me

Two others also, who were criminals, were led away to be put to death with him. When they came to the place that is called The Skull, they crucified Jesus there with the criminals, one on his right and one on his left....One of the criminals who were hanged there kept deriding him and saying, "Are you not the Messiah? Save yourself and us!" But the other rebuked him, saying, "Do you not fear God, since you are under the same sentence of condemnation? And we indeed have been condemned justly, for we are getting what we deserve for our deeds, but this man has done nothing wrong." Then he said, "Jesus, remember me when you come into your kingdom." He replied, "Truly I tell you, today you will be with me in Paradise."

LUKE 23:32–33, 39–43

I f there is any passage which asks the question unequivocally, "Were you there?" it is this one. Jesus is lifted up on the cross in the central place; on his left and right are crucified two thieves; scattered around are soldiers, a few priestly elders and rulers to observe the end, and some common people—all of them representing the lost with whom Jesus spent his life to bring them salvation and healing. And here, on the outskirts of the crowd there are some believing women too—perhaps the most faithful of all. And there, in some shadow, endeavoring not to be too easily seen, stand you and I.

Luke is both sensitive and dramatic in his presentation of the scene, and it is likely that this picture is drawn in order to do that very thing—to draw people like you and me to the cross, in order that we may behold, may reflect, may consider, weep, repent, and even cry, "Jesus, remember me!"

There is one obdurate and one repentant sinner—and Jesus divides them. It is as if he, the reconciler, the redeemer of all, plants his cross at the heart of the world and divides good from evil, the righteous from the wicked, the obdurate from the repentant. The division

122

is made so that it may be clear that a decision is called for. If anyone can look upon the bleeding, suffering Christ, the One whose heart was grieved, and whose soul was burdened with the world's sin, and then cast his ultimate and precious sacrifice back in his face—then that one pronounces judgment upon his or her own soul.

Out of the hubbub of soldiers' mocking, the voice of the impenitent thief is heard. "Call yourself Messiah? You can't even save yourself. The Messiah has power and authority; the Messiah brings salvation, and casts the foreign tyrant out of the land—but you are weak and helpless, hanging on a Roman cross. If you are the Messiah save yourself—and take us with you..." and his mocking and crying turns to gibberish. It is not that the poor creature wants to curse and blaspheme, but he is in extremity. He is suffering too—even to the death—and his Jewish understanding of the Messiah is that he would be a mighty liberator after the manner of the great Judas Maccabeus, gathering the zealot party, supported by the whole populace, enthused and inspired to make Jerusalem again the center of the world. He was not only disappointed, but disillusioned.

Out of the mysterious afternoon darkness comes the voice of the second thief, "Don't shout such blasphemies, man. You and I are in the same mess—the three of us are going to die. We have plundered, robbed and killed—but this man is innocent. This man, in spite of it all, is the Messiah...." And as if he had received the dying grace of revelation, he turned to the man on the central cross and called Jesus by his name, "Jesus, remember me when you come into your kingdom."

Jesus did not answer or rebuke the first thief. He himself was the answer, hanging in sorrow and yet enthroned for those who had eyes to see. But he slowly turned his head towards the penitent thief and gave him such fullness of answer and promise that exceeded anything he could have requested. "Truly I tell you," and the words pierced the thief's heart, "today you will be with me in Paradise."

It was not that Jesus was rejecting the thief who seemed impenitent and obdurate. Given his upbringing, mind-set, and teaching, what else could he say, how else could he react? And it is not ours to pronounce a sentence of final condemnation upon any dying soul. He may have been confronted with the risen Jesus on the other side of Easter, and had the two ways set clearly before him with a real opportunity for decision—the whole truth shining in radiant clarity. If then he would knowingly, deliberately, calculatedly reject the divine love, then he would have chosen his own darkness, but that is between him and the Lord.

What we should observe here is Jesus' acceptance of the repentant thief, and the glorious promise that carried him over the river and into the garden of God's paradise. And all this not on the ground of merit, good works, or human goodness, but simply because he recognized himself as a sinful and helpless soul in the hour of his mortal agony, with no one else to turn to, and only Jesus before him. If any soul manifests the joy of salvation by faith, the lost sheep being found by the shepherd, the prodigal son returning to his yearning father—it is this one.

He called Jesus by his first and saving name—the name of Jesus is the symbol and meaning of our salvation. Every novice who enters Orthodox monastic life on Mount Athos receives a prayer rope and simple instructions on saying the Jesus Prayer: "Lord Jesus Christ, Son of God, have mercy on me, a sinner."

This is the basic prayer I have been saying for over twenty-five years, and the one which will carry me into the arms of my Lord Jesus in life and in death. It is the prayer that sounds continually in my heart, and which enfolds me to his heart—the prayer that lays hold on the saving name of Jesus, and proves it to be the name of the Savior of the world.

Prayer

Jesus, hanging between two thieves: If there is one prayer which rises today, it is "Remember me." If there is one name which sounds the melody of love, it is the name of Jesus. Grant to me a penitent heart in my living, a believing heart in my dying. Lord Jesus Christ, Son of God, have mercy on me, a sinner.

Reflection

There is much to be said about social and political involvement for the sake of the compassion of Christ, but the dying thief was too far gone for all that. In our lives we must give ourselves as Jesus gave himself in the service of others, and for the alleviation of suffering. But there comes a time when we are fixed upon our own cross, when we have nowhere else to go, and no one else to whom we can turn. We must not presume that the Lord will be merciful to us then, though this story tells us of dying grace—but we must prepare ourselves now, so that in our last day we shall be able, with humble confidence, to look into his eyes and pray, "Jesus, remember me."

LENT 5: THURSDAY

Nicodemus: Born From Above

Then the temple police went back to the chief priests and Pharisees, who asked them, "Why did you not arrest him?" The police answered, "Never has anyone spoken like this!" Then the Pharisees replied, "Surely you have not been deceived too, have you? Has any one of the authorities or of the Pharisees believed in him? But this crowd, which does not know the law—they are accursed." Nicodemus, who had gone to Jesus before, and who was one of them, asked, "Our law does not judge people without first giving them a hearing to find out what they are doing, does it?" They replied, "Surely you are not also from Galilee, are you? Search and you will see that no prophet is to arise from Galilee….

JOHN 7:45–52

Nicodemus, who had at first come to Jesus by night, also came, bringing a mixture of myrrh and aloes, weighing about a hundred pounds. They took the body of Jesus and wrapped it with the spices in linen cloths, according to the burial custom of the Jews.

JOHN 19:39–40

S ome people come to conversion suddenly, powerfully, irrevocably. They may use the term "born again," for it certainly seems to them that a wonderful thing has happened: from darkness to light; from sin to righteousness; from Satan to God. This was the experience of Saul on the road to Damascus, and of the blind man who silenced the arguments of the Pharisees by affirming, "One thing I do know, that though I was blind, now I see" (Jn 9:25).

Other people understand their spiritual life as a process; perhaps with moments of insight or even an initiatory decision, but they experience it as a gradual change. It was to Nicodemus that this call to be born again came, and yet he experienced it in a gradual way, and we can see three stages in his appearances in John's Gospel, and that was a reflection of his spirituality.

First, he came to Jesus by night (Jn 3:1–10), somewhat anonymously (he is only mentioned in John's Gospel), a Pharisee, and even a member of the Sanhedrin. Coming by night had nothing to do with the night that enveloped Judas (Jn 13:30). Nicodemus' night had to do with caution because as a member of the ruling Sanhedrin party he was an example, and in any case wanted to make sure of his intuition that this young rabbi's teaching had the ring of truth about it. The rabbis said that night is a good time for study, and as the saying goes, it is easier to pray in a dimly lit church.

He was puzzled, even perplexed, for something was lacking in his religious life of legalism and juridical rules. He sought light in the darkness—in a word, enlightenment. Jesus came straight to the point and did not conduct a seminar or initiate a house group for discussion. It was like the old hymn says:

> *A ruler once came to Jesus by night*
> *to ask him the way of salvation and light;*
> *The master made answer in words true and plain:*
> *"You must be born again."*

But what could Jesus have meant? Nicodemus genuinely misunderstood. It was not that he was resisting truth, but he needed time, preparation, and light from the Holy Spirit. These things were all given along the way, but on this night the basic seeds were sown. He was told that he needed to be born from above—this is what the Greek means. Not just born again, but born from God—a mighty work of the Holy Spirit. And he should have known that Jesus was fulfilling the prophetic yearning expressed in Ezekiel 36:26–27: "A new heart I will give you, and a new spirit I will put within you; and I will remove from your body the heart of stone and give you a heart of flesh. I will put my spirit within you...."

And from his own devotions Nicodemus should have remembered the words of the repentant David after his sin with Bathsheba: "Create in me a clean heart, O God, and put a new and right spirit within me. Do not cast me away from your presence, and do not take your holy spirit from me" (Ps 51:10–11).

When he curiously asked Jesus how it was possible—remember he was an old man, well versed in a respectable codified religion of rules and regulations—he was told that the Holy Spirit was like the wind (the Hebrew word *ruach*, and the Greek word *pneuma* are the same words for wind or spirit). The wind is powerful, spontaneous, effective, and free. It can whisper in the loving mystery of the rustling leaves at night, or it can roar like a gale, leaving a trail of havoc and destruction after it—coming and going at its own behest and known only by its consequences. So is every one who is born of the Spirit.

These were dangerous and life-giving words from a radical preacher of regeneration to a dutiful member of the church establishment. And yet the wind of the Spirit was already breathing in Nicodemus, and the mighty work had begun.

His next appearance is at a meeting of the Sanhedrin which they had set up to trap and condemn Jesus. The temple police returned without arresting Jesus, and gave as the reason that they were bowled over by his mighty words—no one had ever confronted them like this. The Pharisees were angry and contemptuous and said that no intellectual and no one from the religious life had succumbed to him; the common crowd were despicable and they would swallow anything.

It was time for Nicodemus to break his silence, and in the face of anger, contempt, prejudice, and danger he appealed to justice, to humanity, and to common decency, "Our law does not judge people without first giving them a hearing to find out what they are doing, does it?"

But they were not open to reason and flung his gracious intervention back in his face. For them, Jesus' condemnation was a foregone conclusion because he had disturbed the status quo, and was a wild libertarian. As Caiaphas said ironically, but with unconsciously equivocal words, "It is expedient for us, that one man should die for the people" (Jn 11:50, AV).

Nicodemus took a courageous step, for the rest of the Sanhedrin were now in a dangerous mood, and he saw quite clearly that he would now be a marked man and would have to watch his step. Perhaps at this point we would have liked to see him step out with a bold, decisive word of support and approval. But his conversion was not yet complete, and he had another task which was one of the loveliest services ever done for our Lord in his vulnerability and need.

He may have absented himself from the mock trial, or he may have spoken quietly on a personal level to certain members of the Sanhedrin, or even been silent. We do not know. What we do know is that what Jesus' word had begun in his soul, the cross brought to completion. He was drawn to the cross, and the power of the cross brought him to a place of radical decision, where he openly joined with another secret disciple within the Sanhedrin. The two of them took down the body of Jesus from the cross after the horror of the crucifixion, carried it to the garden tomb, prepared it with spices, shroud, and linen, and laid it lovingly in its place with a strange and perplexing hope burning within them.

Whatever the consequences, Nicodemus was now a confessed disciple, even when Jesus' own disciples forsook him in the hour of his deepest distress.

Prayer

Jesus, believed in secretly: Like Nicodemus I feel that my conversion has hardly begun, let alone come to fruition; like Nicodemus, I come to you curious and perplexed, feeling something lacking, and longing for new life; like Nicodemus, I need the powerful and dangerous wind of the Spirit to blow through my life with its spontaneous and life-giving energies. Along the road of my conversion, Lord, let me make that necessary decision to follow you, whatever the cost, in affirmation of my love.

Reflection

Whether you feel your conversion to have been sudden or gradual, the fact remains that you are called into definite discipleship, closer fellowship, and deeper relationship with Jesus. Do not long for other people's experiences, but realize that there may be a secret reason within the heart of God for the way you have been led, and there may be a vocation of loving only you will be able to fulfill. And when the Lord makes his will known, like Nicodemus who was drawn to the cross, you will give your heart and hands to the task.

LENT 5: FRIDAY

Joseph of Arimathea: Preparing the Tomb

Now there was a good and righteous man named Joseph, who, though
a member of the council, had not agreed to their plan and action.
He came from the Jewish town of Arimathea, and he was waiting
expectantly for the kingdom of God. This man went to Pilate and
asked for the body of Jesus. Then he took it down, wrapped it in a
linen cloth, and laid it in a rock-hewn tomb where no one had ever
been laid.

LUKE 23:50–53

I've always had a warm place in my heart for this man. It is not so
much based on evidence as much as circumstances and the nu-
ances of the Gospels. So important is Joseph of Arimathea's person
and deed that although we know little about him, what we do know is
significant beyond mere words, and he is reported in all four gospels.

Some have said that being a member of the Sanhedrin, he could
have intervened (with Nicodemus) on behalf of Jesus at the trial. But
it does look as if Caiaphas handpicked a selected number at what was
a mock trial anyway, and Joseph and Nicodemus were suspect, and
therefore not asked.

Jesus died at 3:00 P.M. on the Friday afternoon, and the high Sabbath began at around 6:00 P.M., so there was little time. The Romans
did not mind leaving bodies on or around the crucifixion site for wild
beasts and birds of prey to scavenge. Perhaps that is why the name
Golgotha means Place of a Skull. But the Jews would not leave a
body on the cross overnight (Deut 21:22–23).

Joseph was a good and righteous man, and he had not consented
to the condemnation of the Sanhedrin. He was one of those devout
Jews who did not look for a Maccabean military conqueror, but a
Messiah who would bring hope and peace—as did Simeon, Anna,
Zachariah, and Elizabeth.

He was a disciple of Jesus, but secretly, adds John (19:38), for fear of the Jews. His nature and temperament was therefore timid, but at this point it is clear that the cross had touched his heart and stirred his will to action, and he conquered his fears. He courageously went to Pilate and begged the body of Jesus.

When Jesus died there was an atmospheric change. The day lightened somewhat and the sun was restored to fading light, as the Sabbath lights began to be lit over the land. In such approaching evening light, we can imagine a conversation taking place between Joseph and Nicodemus. Joseph is in the forefront here, for it was his influence with Pilate, his money, his rock-hewn tomb and his garden in which it lay. Indeed, Joseph may have been the uncle of Mary if the Cornish legend is correct, and if so he may have claimed the relative's right, in Roman law, to claim the body.

The three Synoptic Gospels do not mention Nicodemus at all. There may have been political reasons for this, but in John's Gospel, written some forty years later, the danger may have passed. They certainly would have a lot to share, and this was a common area of their secret counsels, for both were committed to Jesus. It was the event of the cross that drew them closer to him, and therefore to one another.

It must have been a sacred and somewhat frightening experience to take down the body of Jesus from the cross and to carry it gently and tenderly to the garden. It had been vibrant and full of life-giving and healing energy, and now it was inert and cold.

When I was superior here at Glasshampton monastery, we had a team of brothers who were painting the chapel, and I decided that I would go into the sanctuary at about 5:00 A.M., before the brothers were astir, and take down and repaint the corpus of Jesus from the fixed cross on the wall above the altar.

When I went in through the darkness, and slowly began to turn up the dimming lights, I received a sudden shock, and I can feel the scariness of it now. On the raised, stone altar at the east end of the chapel, lay the white corpus of Jesus, nearly six feet in length, with arms outstretched. It took a little time of deep breathing to understand the significance of the dead Christ stretched upon the altar of sacrifice. One of the brothers had taken it down the night before, and omitted to tell me.

Although our Savior is not dead, and not stretched out upon any altar or crucifix now, but alive and radiant in glory, yet during Holy Week, and especially from Good Friday through Holy Saturday, we enter more profoundly into his passion and dying.

I cleaned, washed, and repainted the crucifix in the darkness of that morning with immense tenderness, with quiet devotion, and with prayerful attention, and it has remained an occasion of real significance which is immediately before me today, even as I write. I was there.

Joseph and Nicodemus were there. They carried out the sacred tasks of cleansing the body, and wrapping it in the linen cloths with the aromatic spices between the folds, ready for the later embalming. They had to work in haste lest the soldiers come upon them, but they worked diligently, lovingly, prayerfully. And at last they laid the body upon the prepared slab within the tomb, and quietly left that holy place, rolling the stone into its groove against the tomb's door.

Prayer

Lord Jesus Christ, Son of the living God, who at this evening hour lay in the tomb, and so hallowed the grave to be a bed of hope for all who put their trust in you; give us such sorrow for our sins, which were the cause of your passion, that when our bodies lie in the dust, our souls may live with you for ever (from the Office of Compline).

Reflection

First, let us determine not to leave the tokens of affection for our loved ones until they have died, for flowers and monuments are not life-giving. Then let us reflect upon the secret candle of devotion which had a genuine place in the lives of Joseph and Nicodemus. It was fanned into flame by the healing breeze that blew from the cross, caus-ing them to conquer their natural timidity and come out as strong and courageous disciples. So let us cultivate the quiet flame in the secret place of prayer, and let the light of Christ shine in our lives at every level of family and professional life.

LENT 5: SATURDAY

Waiting Women: Cross and Tomb

The women who had come with [Jesus] from Galilee followed, and they saw the tomb and how his body was laid. Then they returned, and prepared spices and ointments. On the Sabbath they rested according to the commandment....

LUKE 23:55–56

The chief priests and the Pharisees gathered before Pilate and said, "Sir, we remember what that impostor said while he was still alive, "After three days I will rise again." Therefore command the tomb to be made secure until the third day; otherwise his disciples may go and steal him away, and tell the people, "He has been raised from the dead," and the last deception would be worse than the first." Pilate said to them, "You have a guard of soldiers; go, make it as secure as you can." So they went with the guard and made the tomb secure by sealing the stone.

MATTHEW 27:62–66

L ast at the cross and first at the tomb. What a complete devotion in sorrow, and what an amazing discovery in hope. These are the ministering women from Galilee. Matthew and Mark make special mention of Mary Magdalene, Mary the mother of James and Joseph and the mother of the sons of Zebedee. As these women waited patiently at a distance from the cross, Luke comments on the crowd who had come for violent entertainment but now return home beating their breasts (verse 48). Penitence in such people is too much to ask for yet, but certainly there was grief and a deep sense of foreboding. Perhaps this was the preparation for the genuine repentance which came to fruition at the preaching of Peter to these people after Easter, when we read that "those who welcomed his message were baptized"—a wonderful core of believers in the risen Christ (Acts 2:37–42).

But we must stay with sorrow just now, and share with these dedicated women their grief and heaviness—at a distance because either they were not permitted to come any nearer, or because of the awe that filled them. Luke is keen to point out that they "saw" the things that had happened, and could later witness that Jesus really suffered, really died—and that it was no phantom or deceit.

We lose sight of these women when Joseph and Nicodemus come on the scene, but Luke picks up the trail again in verse 55 where again the women saw the tomb and the body, so there would be no mistake when later they came to anoint and embalm. Luke is very careful to make these points, for later, Jesus' enemies would say that there was deceit, gnostics would say that it was not a "real" body, and unbelieving theologians would say that the women made a mistake in identifying the tomb.

Matthew makes the point that Mary Magdalene and her Mary companion were actually there—not in sight of the two men who tenderly brought, wrapped, and laid Jesus in the tomb, but sitting opposite, watching, waiting, contemplating.

I am writing these words at the end of Advent, in the darkness of a frost-laden morning, and have just walked out of my hermitage to the edge of the enclosure, and stood, touching the head of my Brother Francis statue under the cherry tree—it is shining with frost. It is not difficult to imagine Joseph's tomb-garden from this place, or to enter into the contemplative attitude of the women in their waiting sorrow—for it could be here.

How strange it is, and how familiar, that the human heart should wait and prepare for that for which there seems no hope. It is because God was moving within them, taking the initiative for the next amazing move, and preparing these women for the discovery which would explode in a wonder of incredible joy. Incredible is the word—for it is the supreme moment in the whole movement of God's incarnation among us. But for this we must wait with the women.

After the Sabbath preparation, says Matthew, when Joseph, Nicodemus, and the women had departed from the garden, the chief priests and Pharisees deliberately broke their own law and went to Pilate with the ironic request that a guard and seal should be set upon the tomb. It was because, they said, that words had been spoken about

Jesus rising from the dead, and his disciples might perpetrate a great hoax.

Pilate may have smiled wryly at their desperate anxiety to eliminate Jesus entirely—they were certainly obsessed with him. So he said, in effect, "Go on then, take the soldiers, seal and guard the tomb, and make it secure—if you can." But as one of our Easter hymns says, "Vain the stone, the watch, the seal…" for when the Prince of Life is ready, hell will be harrowed, the bronze gates of death will be shattered, and the stone will be rolled away.

But for us today, on the edge of Holy Week, we accompany the women in spirit as they prepare their spices and ointments for the embalming, and rest on the Sabbath day.

Prayer

Jesus, waiting in the tomb: There are times when the sap falls, the light of life is low, and we are enveloped in heaviness, seemingly "at a distance" from your love. In those times, give us the grace of waiting, a period of preparation, the gift of contemplation. The darkness will give way to dawn, and the Sun of Righteousness will arise in our hearts—if we believe and hold fast.

Reflection

How divided is the world, dramatically portrayed at the foot of the cross: the jeering chief priests and elders, the crowd who came for entertainment, the soldiers doing their duty, the women at a distance— a handful of loyal believers now pressed sorely in their sadness. There will always be enemies of Jesus at the cross, bent on eliminating love and humanity in our world. Our task is to be faithful in the darkness, to bear witness to the light of compassion wherever it may manifest itself, and to wait for the coming dawn.

—— ✠ ——

Holy Week

———✠———

Seven Words From the Cross

PALM SUNDAY

First Word: Father, Forgive

When they came to the place that is called The Skull, they crucified
Jesus there with the criminals, one on his right and one on his left.
Then Jesus said, "Father, forgive them; for they do not know what
they are doing."

LUKE 23:32–38

On Palm Sunday we stand at a place where we pause, take a deep
breath, and consider the whole seven days before us—the most
dramatic week in the story of the world's redemption. The one word
which breathes through the whole narrative and which redeems the
terrible violence, hatred, and cruelty is this word: *Forgiveness*.

The tears of Jesus as he approached Jerusalem indicate the sorrow in the heart of God because of humankind's rejection and alienation, and his words are variously translated, "If you only knew…if
you only understood…if you only recognized…" (Lk 19:42). Bishop
William Walsham How's children's hymn touches the very heart of
the gospel when he writes of the wonder of God's dear Son coming,
toiling, dying for us poor sinners, and he goes on:

> *But even could I see him die,*
> *I could but see a little part*
> *Of that great love which, like a fire,*
> *Is always burning in his heart.*

That's the center of it all—the love which was manifest in the
suffering Savior on the cross with arms outstretched in sorrow. And
that picture is the historical enactment of the love which eternally
burns in the heart of the Father.

The implications and unfolding of what happened at Calvary take
us into the deep waters of overwhelming grace and divinity. But it
begins for us in that word *forgiveness*, and the tears of Jesus, seated
on the donkey, before his descent to Jerusalem.

We begin today the seven words from the cross, and this first one sets the scene and reveals the heart and attitude of Christ towards those who nail him to the cross, and can then be seen in ever-widening circles out to the whole world.

Forgiveness is not cheap, and Jesus is beginning to pay the price of it in this terrible deed done by common soldiers under orders. It is so easy for us to indulge in a kind of "armchair forgiveness" when we are not hurt, wounded, persecuted, or hated in a malicious or fatal manner. Or even to forgive on behalf of others when we have not directly been affected. That, of course, is not really possible, for you can only forgive if you have been the victim.

I am at present reading *The Lost Art of Forgiving*, published by the Anabaptist and Hutterite Bruderhof Community (Plough Publishing, Robertsbridge, 1998), who maintain their pacifist witness with their feet firmly on the ground, while remaining open to all people of compassion. On the cover is that famous, but horrific, picture of the naked nine-year-old girl, napalm-burned, crying, arms outstretched, running towards the camera with plumes of black smoke billowing behind her.

It came from the napalm raid on the village of Tran Gang in Vietnam in 1972, and the name of the little girl was Phan Thi Kim Phuc. The helicopter pilot who organized the raid was John Plummer, who is now a Methodist minister in Virginia. For the next twenty years he was haunted by that picture and the consequences of what he had done.

The story of his meeting Kim in 1996 at the Vietnam Memorial on Veterans' Day is told in the book, among other amazing and wonderful stories of forgiveness. We catch a glimpse:

> Kim saw my grief, my pain, my sorrow...she held out her arms to me and embraced me. All I could say was "I'm sorry; I'm sorry"—over and over again. And at the same time she was saying, "It's all right, I forgive you."

Kim forgave John, and John began to tread the long path of forgiving himself and dedicating himself, with Kim, to promote peace and reconciliation. There is an insert photograph, at the bottom of that large cover picture of Kim and John, heads together in smiling joy—but not without the tears of the decades between them. Forgiveness is costly, and as I read this story, I could hear the words of Jesus, and the grace that he gives to those who seek mercy, "Father, forgive them, for they do not know what they are doing."

Prayer

Jesus, forgiving Savior: There have been times when I have known very well what I have been doing, and have still done it. And yet I have never known the pain and grief that my sins cause to your loving heart. Enable me to understand the ways of true repentance, forgiveness, and reconciliation, and let them guide my life and relationships.

Reflection

Think now. Are there still those you have never forgiven, and who have never forgiven you? Is it possible to take one simple step today to heal such a relationship? And could this lead to a whole new attitude in your life? If so, it is your privilege and joy to seek God's grace to put such wheels in motion.

—— ✚ ——

HOLY WEEK: MONDAY

Second Word: Paradise Today

One of the criminals who were hanged there kept deriding him and saying, "Are you not the Messiah? Save yourself and us!" But the other rebuked him, saying, "Do you not fear God, since you are under the same sentence of condemnation? And we indeed have been condemned justly, for we are getting what we deserve for our deeds, but this man has done nothing wrong." Then he said, "Jesus, remember me when you come into your kingdom." He replied, "Truly I tell you, today you will be with me in Paradise."

LUKE 23:39–43

We looked at the story of the penitent thief last Wednesday, and marveled at the amazing grace which was in full flood right in the middle of the horror, agony, and darkness of the cross—assuring us that if ever we should be transfixed in a place of no hope in this life, there is One to whom we can turn in our utter, absolute and terminal need. And he will be there.

But today there are two things we should consider, focusing not upon the thief but upon the Savior. They are the crucifixion itself, and the mysterious "light in darkness" which was the experience of Jesus, and which penetrated, ultimately, even the darkest, lowest, most terrible episode of desolation which we shall consider on Wednesday.

None of the evangelists dwell on the cruelty and personal agony which Jesus underwent. There is even restraint and austerity about it. But the awful, grim, and terrible fact is there before us: a man on a cross. The evangelists are concerned with the effects and consequences of the cross—upon the crowd and upon the reader of the narrative. As if they are asking, "Were *you* there?" and going on to affirm that we were all there, all responsible, all drawn into the terror, the mystery, and the redemption accomplished at Calvary. In his book *Crucifixion* (SCM Press, 1977), the German theologian Martin Hengel writes of such an effect:

By the public display of a naked victim at a prominent place—
at a crossroads, in the theater, on high ground, at the place of
his crime—crucifixion also represented his uttermost humili-
ation, which had a numinous dimension to it. With Deu-
teronomy 21:23 in the background, the Jew in particular was
very aware of this. This form of execution, more than any
other, had associations with the idea of human sacrifice, which
was never completely suppressed in antiquity….In Roman
times crucifixion was practiced above all on dangerous criminals and members of the lowest classes….Because large strata
of the population welcomed the security and the worldwide
peace which the empire brought with it, the crucified victim
was defamed both socially and ethically in popular awareness, and this impression was heightened still further by the
religious elements involved.

This is the scandal and stumbling block of which Paul writes (1 Cor
1:23), when he talks of the divine foolishness in setting forth the cross
as manifesting the love, power, and wisdom of God in his beloved
Son.

The thief, in his own agony, turned and gazed upon the central
crucified man and through the horror of the place of no escape, he
received an illumination in which foolishness became wisdom. He
saw there a king, exalted upon his throne, regal in his dying, clothed
in the naked majesty of suffering love, and he cried out, "Jesus, remember me when you come into your kingdom."

This underlines the second of our considerations: that Jesus received and manifested the light of glory in the midst of his darkness
and suffering. When this poor, dying thief cried out to him from the
depths—deep calling unto deep—Jesus responded with a mysterious
confidence, in words which assured the thief not only that he was
king, but that he would lead him into the fellowship of his heavenly
kingdom.

None of this denies the very real agony and suffering, the loneli-
ness, darkness, and abandonment that were part of Jesus' descent into

the hell of dereliction for our sakes. But it does mean that we can sink to no depths that he has not plumbed, and that he has suffered such abandonment and dereliction that we may never be left ultimately alone.

Prayer

Jesus, enthroned on the cross: Grant me the penitence, the enlightenment, and the faith shown by the dying thief. In my last hour may I cry, "Jesus, remember me!" and hear your words of assurance, "Paradise today."

Reflection

We are redeemed by the same grace that was extended to the dying thief. But unlike him we have a life to live on earth, in order that others may be drawn to the love that embraces all humankind.

HOLY WEEK: TUESDAY

Third Word:
Woman, Behold Your Son

Standing near the cross of Jesus were his mother, and his mother's sister, Mary the wife of Clopas, and Mary Magdalene. When Jesus saw his mother and the disciple whom he loved standing beside her, he said to his mother, "Woman, here is your son." Then he said to the disciple, "Here is your mother." And from that hour the disciple took her into his own home.

JOHN 19:25–27

B ecause I have lived in the grounds of the monastery dedicated to Saint Mary at the Cross, I feel a special nearness to this moving episode at the cross of Jesus. People often say that when they walk (or drive) up the rugged track to Glasshampton, they feel as if they are making a pilgrimage, and when they arrive at the gate, they are faced with the words below the tower, "At the cross of Jesus stood his mother." This hymn I wrote for our special day spells out its meaning:

SAINT MARY AT THE CROSS

See Mary standing at the cross
On which her Son and Savior dies,
Deep sadness wrings her wounded heart,
Compassion fills her sorrowing eyes.

John, the disciple Jesus loves
Stands firm, unflinching, at her side;
And leaning on each other's grief
They gaze upon the Crucified.

Then Jesus, hanging on the cross
Speaks through his tears and sweat
and blood,

144

Commending Mary to John's care,
And John unto her motherhood.

We also stand beneath the cross
And share in John and Mary's pain;
Lord, open wide our hearts and minds,
To hear your blessed words again.

Your mother's love and John's strong prayers
Will intercede before your throne,
And we, with them, shall see your face
When you will gather home your own.

Lord Jesus, all your pain is done,
The empty cross and open grave
Proclaim your strong, redeeming love
For those you died and rose to save.

No more with Mary at the cross,
But robed in light, in heaven above,
With her we'll lift up heart and voice,
And bless you for your saving love.

We have already thought about John at the foot of the cross, and the Saturday before last about Mary at the foot of the cross. Today we focus on Jesus himself. The wonderful thing is that in the midst of his own agony and pain he had eyes and heart for his mother, and for the beloved disciple.

If this was so, how can we doubt that he has a place for us today at the foot of the cross? A few days ago, Gill from Glasgow came to see me, and as we knelt in my chapel we both gazed upon the Franciscan crucifix. "It is remarkable," she said, "that so many people surround the cross; that with us there are always others…" and we spoke of the communion of saints. The cross itself "draws" people as a magnet of divine love, and the common bond of love and sacrifice is the mark of God's people. There is a great cloud of witnesses there, and in glory, and yet it is as if I am the only one, and that Jesus cares simply for me.

Jesus gave his beloved disciple into the care of his mother. I remember this when I hear the monastery Angelus bell ring, and the prayer arises from our hearts: "Hail Mary, full of grace, the Lord is with you; blessed are you among women, and blessed is the fruit of your womb, Jesus...."

And Jesus gave his mother into the care of his beloved disciples. At this moment Mary is called "Mother of sorrows"—Simeon's prophecy of the pierced heart had at last been fulfilled, and we care for Jesus' mother by entering with her into that maternal grief in which she can only stand and watch and wait.

Stand and watch and wait for what? Well, there is something in this scene that indicates that it is not the end. There is something in Mary's heart which tells her that the pain and agony of Calvary is the penultimate word—the ultimate word is with love—with God. She can only hope, only reach out in faith, only weep in the tender loyalty that roots her to this very spot. But it is from this patient attitude of simple passivity that hope springs up, and the light which shines from the empty tomb illuminates her inward grief.

Prayer

Jesus, son of Mary: In tenderness you cared for your beloved disciple and mother while hanging on the cross; in tenderness you care for me in my griefs and joys. Let me care for you and for your mother in reaching out to alleviate the sufferings of the needy.

Reflection

There is a time for grieving. Holy Week is the time, and Calvary is the place. But let hope be rekindled in the midst of grief, and do not allow grief to become self-pity or lead to despair. We may not today feel the joy of Easter rising, but it is not too far ahead. Only believe.

— ✤ —

HOLY WEEK: WEDNESDAY

Fourth Word: My God, My God

From noon on, darkness came over the whole land until three in the afternoon. And about three o'clock Jesus cried with a loud voice, "Eli, Eli, lema sabachthani?" that is, "My God, my God, why have you forsaken me?" When some of the bystanders heard it, they said, "This man is calling for Elijah." At once one of them ran and got a sponge, filled it with sour wine, put it on a stick, and gave it to him to drink. But the others said, "Wait, let us see whether Elijah will come to save him."

MATTHEW 27:45–49

There is no more terrible, more mysterious, more numinous words in the whole of the gospel story than those found in this fourth word from the cross, "My God, my God, why have you forsaken me?"

Jesus was crucified at nine o'clock, and he died at three o'clock in the afternoon, and during those last three hours the very cosmos itself seemed to be in mourning, for the sun was darkened, and out of the unrelieved gloom of this most terrible day in the story of the world, this cry ascends.

What is happening here? Ultimately, we do not know, and there is a sense in which it may be right for us to fall on our faces in awe and wonder, because in some strange way the Son cries out in utter abandonment and dereliction, and the Father seems to hide his face in the moment of deepest darkness and universal loss. But even these words have been given us, so that we may glimpse into the nature of sin, the character of God, and the wonder of the divine love.

It may be, as some have thought, that Jesus was speaking out, in his hour of darkness, the words of the twenty-second psalm which he had known from childhood. If Jesus found some comfort in these ancient words it would be a help to us, for the desolation of the psalm breaks out of suffering at last, into hope, and even triumph (Ps 22:19–31).

But Jesus is not here simply repeating the words of some other sufferer. He is crying out from the depths of his own desolation, from an experience which has never been his before, and from such darkness as no one else has ever known, or can ever know.

In preparation for writing this chapter, I have been listening to Bach's *Saint Matthew Passion*, and especially the repetition of the Passion Chorale:

> *O sacred head, sore wounded,*
> *With grief and pain weighed down,*
> *How scornfully surrounded*
> *With thorns, thine only crown!*
> *How pale thou art with anguish,*
> *With sore abuse and scorn!*
> *How does that visage languish*
> *Which once was bright as morn!*

In such an image of the crucified Son of God we see Jesus descending to the deepest depth of human suffering, bereft of all help and comfort, plumbing the depths of the human situation of desolation and alienation—further than we can ever go. This means that Jesus scaled the highest heights and descended to the deepest depths—and all for us.

But there is even more—and this is the place where we have to be still in wonder and fear. Jesus had embodied compassion and mercy in his life; had sympathized with human suffering at every level; had imparted hope and healing. But never, never before had he encountered in himself the experience and consequences of human sin.

It is at this place that Jesus uttered those terrible words of dereliction. The consequences of bearing our sin identified him totally with humankind, and in some mysterious way, that meant alienation from God, separation from the loving Father, and absolute and utter desolation.

Even as I write these words I wonder if this could have been possible and if it could possibly have meant such a thing. It seems like a contradiction, and it has implications that I shy away from—a rift within the nature of God—and that makes me tremble, and I move back from such an interpretation.

But these are those awful words, and if they were the final words I think that the tears which are just below the surface as I write would reveal my own desolation—and I have only glimpsed the meaning.

But if it is not a contradiction, it is certainly a paradox. That the eternal Word could become a mortal child is paradox; that the Son of God could hang upon a cross is paradox; that the holy and sinless One could bear human sin is a paradox. And the whole amazing paradox is summed up in the fact that it is God who has become incarnate among his people. It is God himself who takes upon himself the griefs, sorrows, and burdens of humankind. It is God himself who suffers, bleeds, and dies for sinners, for "in Christ God was reconciling the world to himself, not counting their trespasses against them" (2 Cor 5:19).

If this is true it makes us tremble. But not now in fear and terror, but in profound gratitude and in tearful, tender joy. I say that these were not the final words, but they are the words which have taken us deeper than we have ever explored before, or can ever fully understand in our mortal lives.

Prayer

Jesus, in desolation and dereliction: When I sink to my lowest ebb, know my deepest sorrow, and come to my time of dying, do not hide your face from me. You have suffered such darkness in order that in my dark valley the light may shine. Thank you, my dear Savior.

Reflection

If today's words were truly spoken, really experienced, and our Lord came through the ultimate darkness, then there is not only hope for us, but for all those who come with their burdens and sins. No one need now be completely desolate or absolutely abandoned, because Christ not only wholly understands, but has wholly experienced the darkest hell. And he is our Savior.

MAUNDY THURSDAY

Fifth Word: I Thirst

After this, when Jesus knew that all was now finished, he said (in order to fulfill the scripture), "I am thirsty." A jar full of sour wine was standing there. So they put a sponge full of the wine on a branch of hyssop and held it to his mouth.

JOHN 19:28–29

In our refectory at Glasshampton monastery, where we eat and drink in silence, there is a crucifix on the facing wall, and beneath it in red is the Latin word *sitio*, which means "I thirst." Jesus spoke these words out of his human thirst and dryness when hanging on the cross, but they also bear a deeper, mystical meaning of his thirst for the souls of men and women. Hymn writer Cecil Frances Alexander relates this paradox to all human suffering and to the work of redemption:

> *His are the thousand sparkling rills*
> *That from a thousand fountains burst,*
> *And fill with music all the hills:*
> *And yet he says, "I thirst."*

> *All fiery pangs on battlefields,*
> *On fever beds where sick men toss,*
> *Are in that human cry he yields*
> *To anguish on the Cross.*

> *But more than pains that racked him then*
> *Was the deep longing thirst divine*
> *That thirsted for the souls of all:*
> *Dear Lord! and one was mine.*

In the final stanza is the prayer that the thirst that Jesus felt in himself and suffered for us may impart to us a thirst for his love, and for the salvation of the world.

The meaning of the fifth word, "I thirst" is all there in C. F. Alexander's hymn. Yet there are two moments in our Lord's ministry that may inspire us as we thirst to love and serve him. The first is when the Samaritan woman came to the well and Jesus asked her for a drink. During the conversation, which led to her salvation, Jesus said, "Everyone who drinks of this water will be thirsty again, but those who drink of the water that I will give them will never be thirsty. The water that I will give will become in them a spring of water gushing up to eternal life" (Jn 4:13–14).

The second moment was when Jesus stood before the crowds on the great day of the festival in Jerusalem, and cried out: "Let anyone who is thirsty come to me, and let the one who believes in me drink. As the Scripture has said, "Out of the believer's heart shall flow rivers of living water" (Jn 7:37–38).

The Greek text does not use the word for heart, but the word *koilia*, which should be translated "belly" or "gut," and which indicates the innermost being. The promise means that the Holy Spirit shall dwell, not only as the innermost source within the believer, but shall spring forth, gush out, overflow. The evangelist says that this can only happen when the Holy Spirit is given in fullness, and that is in the future—a post-Easter promise.

It is also, therefore, in the future for us, because it is Holy Week. We have to stand silently, prayerfully at the foot of the cross, and hear our Lord's words, "I thirst."

Prayer

Jesus, thirsting for the world's salvation: Create in me a thirst which can be satisfied by your love alone; let me thirst for more of your grace, more of your mercy, more of your joy. Then pour the water of life upon and within me, that it may be a river of living water, irrigating the dry land around.

Reflection

We cannot create or pour out the living water. But we can dig the irrigation channels, and pray for the living water to be poured forth.

GOOD FRIDAY

Sixth Word: It Is Finished

[Jesus] looked up to heaven and said, "Father, the hour has come; glorify your Son so that the Son may glorify you, since you have given him authority over all people, to give eternal life to all whom you have given him. And this is eternal life, that they may know you, the only true God, and Jesus Christ whom you have sent. I glorified you on earth by finishing the work that you gave me to do. So now, Father, glorify me in your own presence with the glory that I had in your presence before the world existed."

JOHN 17:1–5

When Jesus had received the wine, he said, "It is finished." Then he bowed his head and gave up his spirit.

JOHN 19:30

This is a word of victory, and in the Greek text (as in the Aramaic that Jesus spoke) it is only one word, *tetelestai*, and it could be rendered, "Accomplished."

After being handed over, and allowing wicked men to do their worst in hating, betraying, and nailing him to the cross, Jesus now takes the initiative in his dying. He is not sobbing or babbling in fear, despair, or even resigned acceptance, crying, "It's the end—I can't take any more...." Rather it is a cry of triumph, of glory, of strange victory, "*Tetelestai.*"

This word could be written over the whole of John's Gospel, for this is the story he had to tell from the beginning. The cross of shame has become the instrument of salvation, and the tree of death has become the tree of life, with its leaves for the healing of the nations (see also Ezek 47:12; Rev 22:2).

We may link this sixth word from the cross with the opening verses of Jesus' high priestly prayer (Jn 17:1 and following), where he says that his hour has come; he has revealed the Father's glory; his work is finished. And so he longs to return to that pre-incarnate glory—the glory of the Father's effulgence and love. This is a prayer of profound yearning; the task is coming to completion and the Son is going home.

After the sixth word, the text goes on to say, "Then he bowed his head and gave up his spirit." Listen to the commentator John Marsh's perceptive words on this text:

> Even at the moment of dying John uses active verbs. There is no "passion" in John; even death is an act for Jesus. In this he is companion with all the synoptists, who also state the event of his death in active verbs (he breathed his last, or yielded up his spirit). But it appears that John's account can be both nearer to the actual facts of death by crucifixion as well as more noticeably indicative of Jesus' initiative. It appears that in crucifixion the condemned person found that as his body tired he was increasingly unable to keep his chest in a position in which breathing was easy and effective. The tendency was to become increasingly unable to press upwards from the feet, so as to keep the chest in a position where, by holding the head upright, breathing could be properly carried on. It was possibly for these reasons that the legs of criminals crucified were broken: once that were done the crucified could no longer press upward from his feet, and his body would sink down and make breathing impossible. What John's account seems to indicate is that Jesus did not succumb passively to death by crucifixion, but rather deliberately chose the moment of his death by bowing his head, thus restricting his breathing, and causing life to become extinct. So even in his physical death he was an agent, as he certainly is set forth as the agent of his death in a wider sense and frame of reference. Again, if this be a feasible comment, the reader has benefitted from John's uncanny eye for the symbolic incident to light up an historical occasion with its proper meaning.
>
> JOHN MARSH, SAINT JOHN (PENGUIN, 1968)

The three Synoptists tell us that Jesus died with a great shout upon his lips (Mt 27:50; Mk 15:37; Lk 23:46), but John tells us that cry was, *"Tetelestai"* This was the shout before the end—an assurance for Jesus, communicated to us with Johannine joy, and it sounds in our ears and heart as we wait for the last breathing of ultimate faith in the seventh word.

Prayer

Jesus, whose task was accomplished: My life's task may have been contradicted from the start; or it may be that I have turned aside on the way; it may be half done; it may almost be complete. I don't really know, but what I ask today is that I may come to a clearer vision, and that my feet may be firmly set upon the right way. So then, at the last, I may be able to say, "It is finished."

Reflection

Can such victory come out of such defeat? Can the broken body on the cross tell any other story than failure and contradiction? The whole message of the gospel says it can—and does. Do I really believe it? And is my life in accordance with such a revelation?

HOLY SATURDAY

Seventh Word: Father, Into Your Hands

It was now about noon, and darkness came over the whole land
until three in the afternoon, while the sun's light failed; and the
curtain of the temple was torn in two. Then Jesus, crying with a
loud voice, said "Father, into your hands I commend my spirit."
Having said this, he breathed his last.

E very night before Compline, I recite the names of those who are
seriously ill, in silence before God. Then I lift them up in the
arms of faith and love, especially in the words which are repeated
during Compline, "Father, into your hands I commend my spirit."

During this year I have had reason to look mortality in the face
and repeat these words with even greater attention and meaning, and
Holy Saturday is the day of days to repeat this prayer. It is Holy Saturday as I write. My early meditation is mostly the Jesus Prayer, leading
into silent waiting on God. This morning it was within the quietness
of the tomb where Jesus' body lay waiting....

At about 5:15 A.M. the dawn chorus began, and I heard the two
little cats who sleep beneath my hermitage stir. Now I have finished
my meditation time and dawn has broken. I brew up some tea and go
out into my enclosure. The birds are quieter, the cherry blossom tree
blooms with great glory, and the fields behind it drop down to the
woodlands, shrouded in morning mist.

I am struck with the difference in the feeling of the day. Yesterday,
in beautiful spring sunshine I took my Celtic cross with the *Stations
of the Cross* booklet, and traversed the fifteen stations around the
lower field, hanging the cross on a branch at each station where I
paused, sang, read, prayed, and journeyed on. The feel of the day was
so different, for especially between 9:00 A.M. and 3:00 P.M. the sorrows and agony of the cross were to the forefront of my praying.

But this morning all is still, waiting, hoping—and because I am
an Easter Christian—expecting. But I must not anticipate too much,

but live in the emptiness, silence, and quiet melancholy of Holy Saturday, remembering the seventh word from the cross, "Father, into your hands I commend my spirit."

In recording this word Luke also makes us see how Jesus' dying affected the witnesses around the cross. The centurion speaks words of Jesus' innocence—in this he joins the unusual company of Pilate, Herod, and the penitent thief. Even the crowd which came for entertainment is moved and saddened. They return home beating their breasts in sorrow. Luke's last words are for Jesus' friends and the women who stood at a distance, watching, waiting, hoping. That is where Luke ends his narrative, before Joseph of Arimathea comes to take down, anoint, and lay the body of Jesus in his garden tomb.

So here on Holy Saturday we have come to the end of our days of Lent, as we shall one day come to the end of the days of our life. Tomorrow's light already filters through, but we must take Holy Saturday seriously, and we can do it by repeating the seventh word, at the foot of the cross, leading into the prayer.

Prayer

My Savior, in my hour of mortal anguish,
When earth grows dim, and round me falls the night,
O breathe your peace, as flesh and spirit languish;
At that dread eventide let there be light.
To your dear cross then turn my eyes in dying;
Lay then your fainting head upon my breast;
Those outstretched arms receive my latest sighing;
And then, dear Lord, your everlasting rest.

Reflection

In the silence of Holy Saturday let us wait alone, with our sisters and brothers in faith, for the Easter light to dawn. Let us offer thanks for all we have learned and experienced during these days of Lent, and with open hearts allow the Lord to lead us into the future of his will.

Easter Day

—✛—

When He Rose Up From the Tomb

EASTER DAY

When He Rose Up From the Tomb

After the Sabbath, as the first day of the week was dawning, Mary Magdalene and the other Mary went to see the tomb. And suddenly there was a great earthquake; for an angel of the Lord, descending from heaven, came and rolled back the stone and sat on it. His appearance was like lightning, and his clothing white as snow. For fear of him the guards shook and became like dead men. But the angel said to the women, "Do not be afraid; I know that you are looking for Jesus who was crucified. He is not here; for he has been raised, as he said. Come, see the place where he lay. Then go quickly and tell his disciples, 'He has been raised from the dead, and indeed he is going ahead of you to Galilee; there you will see him.' ...So they left the tomb quickly with fear and great joy, and ran to tell his disciples. Suddenly Jesus met them and said, 'Greetings!' And they came to him, took hold of his feet, and worshiped him. Then Jesus said to them, 'Do not be afraid; go and tell my brothers to go to Galilee; there they will see me.' "

MATTHEW 28:1–10

The trembling day has come. For the friars and guests assembled in the darkness around a brazier in the monastery walled garden on Easter morning, it begins with the lighting of the new fire, and the lifting up of the great paschal candle, with the cry: "Christ is risen!"

I call it a trembling day because as the folk spiritual sings of the trembling before the crucified Jesus, the trembling now becomes the dancing of a people set free. Trembling of a completely new order, for now we tremble with inebriation and joy.

Over and over again the question has sounded: "Were you there?" And with increasing sorrow we have had to acknowledge that every one of us was there, taking our part, sharing our responsibility in the crucifying of the world's Savior. It was sin that nailed him to the cross— but it was love that kept him there.

Trembling fear and dread fell upon the soldiers guarding the tomb. But when the angel proclaimed the amazing words that the tomb was empty and Jesus was alive, the women were filled with trembling fear and great joy—a wonderful mingling of awe and glory.

All the pain and sorrow of our Lenten darkness is over. The Sun of Righteousness has risen with healing and joy, and this morning that light breaks into the world's darkness for those who believe.

The wonderful thing about this motif of trembling is that it not only evokes adoration, but it promotes humility. We are the Easter people and Jesus is our song, but we are not to become triumphalist in an arrogant or exclusivist mode. We must continue a trembling people, remaining open and loving with all those who cannot yet believe.

Jesus is alive, and we tremble before him. Jesus is in the midst and the trembling power of the Holy Spirit spreads itself among us. Jesus is risen today in our lives, in our church community and in our world, and we tremble in celebration.

So let us sing the spiritual again, and let the implications of the last refrain reverberate with joy:

Oh, sometimes it causes me to tremble, tremble, tremble;
Were you there when he rose up from the tomb?

Prayer

Jesus, risen in glory: We have certainly been there, sharing some of the harrowing darkness and suffering of the last forty days. This morning the light has broken through, and you have risen, not only from the imprisonment of the tomb, but within our heart's yearning. Let your light increase, let your risen life irradiate our own, so that the shining of your resurrection may herald your coming in glory.

Reflection

Suffering and enmity continue in our world, but a new principle has been introduced. Jesus has risen from the dead and revealed that the ultimate word is with love. That principle of new life is active within us, and we must let it shine at every level of our daily lives, in the sure hope that the risen Lord will one day return in glory, and the whole world will be transfigured in his reconciling love.

Appendix

Material for Group Study

T he "shape" of your group meeting will depend on the venue and the kind of people involved. The following format and suggestions may be helpful to the leader and group. The numbered items under the appropriate weeks relate to the following key format:

1. Call to stillness, and short sentence from Scripture.
2. Hymn, if appropriate (see note, below).
3. Lord's Prayer and prayer on the theme.
4. Scripture reading, from the week's material.
5. Presentation, by chosen group member (prepared beforehand from questions, or member's own material).
6. Open discussion, using the proposed questions.
7. Some minutes of shared silence (or meditative music).
8. The Grace of our Lord Jesus Christ... (said by leader or group).

Note: It might be a refreshing change to use some of the older hymns this Lent.

FIRST MEETING:
BEGINNING: CHURCH AND STATE

1. Let us be still in the presence of God... Pilate said... "Then what should I do with Jesus who is called the Messiah?" (Mt 27:22).
2. Hymn, if appropriate.
3. As our Savior taught us, we are bold to say: "Our Father..." Prayer: Heavenly Father, let the light of your Holy Spirit illuminate the word of your Scripture, and shine in our minds and hearts as we wait upon you; through Jesus Christ, Our Lord. Amen.
4. Scripture (from the week's readings).

5. Presentation by a group member.
6. Suggested discussion questions:

- If you were Pilate, what could you have done? What would you have done?
- What big political changes would you make if you could during Lent?
- What big religious changes would you make if you could during Lent?
- Does this week's material move you towards some practical action in your own church or neighborhood?

SECOND MEETING:
LENT 1: JOHN, THE BELOVED

1. Let us be still in the presence of God... "From the cloud came a voice that said, "This is my Son, my Chosen; listen to him." When the voice had spoken, Jesus was found alone (Lk 9:35–36).
2. Hymn, if appropriate.
3. As our Savior taught us, we are bold to say: "Our Father..." Prayer: Lord Jesus, you called your disciple John from the nets, to become an inspired apostle and evangelist; may we hear your call, receive your inspiration, and do your will in our lives. Amen.
4. Scripture (from the week's readings).
5. Presentation by a group member.
6. Suggested discussion questions:

- Which section on John do you most identify with, and why? Church's witness today? In which ways?
- Does John's conversion from "son of thunder" to "apostle of love" help you in your discipleship? How?
- What practical help does this section encourage the Church to offer to the community?

Third Meeting:
Lent 2: Peter, the Rock

1. Let us be still in the presence of God… "As [Jesus] walked by the Sea of Galilee, he saw…Simon…called Peter, casting a net into the sea….And he said…"Follow me, and I will make you fish for people" (Mt 4:18–19).
2. Hymn, if appropriate.
3. As our Savior taught us, we are bold to say: "Our Father…" Prayer: Lord Jesus, you called Peter to be your apostle and leader of your chosen band; through your grace he overcame his weakness, proclaimed your gospel, led your people, and laid down his life for your sake. Grant us a like conversion, courage and faith. Amen.
4. Scripture (from the week's readings).
5. Presentation by a group member.
6. Suggested discussion questions:

    -   Which section on Peter do you most identify with, and why?
    -   Does Peter as a disciple inspire the Church's witness today? In which ways?
    -   Does the basic honesty of Peter's record of affirmation and denial appeal to you? Why?
    -   What agencies of compassion in the community does this section draw you to support? Do you (or your church community) support any such agency?

Fourth Meeting:
Lent 3: Judas, the Traitor

1. Let us be still in the presence of God… "[Judas] approached Jesus to kiss him; but Jesus said to him, 'Judas, is it with a kiss that you are betraying the Son of Man?' " (Lk 22:47–48).
2. Hymn, if appropriate.
3. As our Savior taught us, we are bold to say: "Our Father…" Prayer: Lord Jesus, you were betrayed in the house of your friends, and given over into the hands of wicked men to be crucified; have

mercy upon our denials and betrayals by words and silences; grant us the grace to follow you to our life's end, and preserve us from the last enemy. Amen.

4. Scripture (from the week's readings).
5. Presentation by a group member.
6. Suggested discussion questions:

- Does the Judas story perplex, worry, or disturb you? If so, why?
- What do you feel about Judas's motivation?
- Is there ultimate hope of repentance and forgiveness for Judas? If so, on what basis?
- Who are the Judas characters in our church, community, and state? What can we do about them?

FIFTH MEETING:
LENT 4: MARY, HIS MOTHER

1. Let us be still in the presence of God… "Simeon blessed them and said to his mother Mary, 'This child is destined for the falling and the rising of many in Israel, and to be a sign that will be opposed so that the inner thoughts of many will be revealed—and a sword will pierce your own soul too'" (Lk 2:34–35).
2. Hymn, if appropriate.
3. As our Savior taught us, we are bold to say: "Our Father…" Prayer: Lord Jesus, your mother lived in constant trust and obedience, with both joy and sorrow mingling in her heart; may we bear you within our souls, be obedient to your word, and give birth to your love and compassion in the world of human suffering. Amen.
4. Scripture (from the week's readings).
5. Presentation by a group member.

6. Suggested discussion questions:

- Which section on Mary do you most identify with, and why?
- Does Mary as a disciple inspire the Church's witness today? In which ways?
- Does Mary strike you most as passive or active? In which ways?
- What place should Mary have in our theology and practice of Christian life and prayer?

SIXTH MEETING:
LENT 5: DRAWN TO THE CROSS

1. Let us be still in the presence of God… "As they led [Jesus] away, they seized a man, Simon of Cyrene, who was coming from the country, and they laid the cross on him, and made him carry it behind Jesus" (Lk 23:26).
2. Hymn, if appropriate.
3. As our Savior taught us, we are bold to say: "Our Father…" Prayer: Lord Jesus, as you walked the way of sorrows, Simon was compelled to carry your cross, mysteriously drawn to it by love; may we recognize that our crossbearing may be taken up into your greater plan of love, and at last be grateful for the burdens we have borne for you. Amen.
4. Scripture (from the week's readings).
5. Presentation by a group member.
6. Suggested discussion questions:

- Which of the characters in this section do you most identify with, and why?
- Was the cross of Jesus indispensable to the people in this section, or could they have come to him some other way?
- Are there different ways of responding to the gospel (for example, secret discipleship, public witness, different lifestyles)? Which is your way?
- Is it possible to "stand at a distance" all your life, and enter into the kingdom of God at last?

SEVENTH MEETING:
HOLY WEEK: SEVEN WORDS FROM THE CROSS

1. Let us be still in the presence of God… "When they came to the place that is called The Skull, they crucified Jesus there with the criminals, one on his right, and one on his left (Lk 23:33).
2. Hymn, if appropriate.
3. As our Savior taught us, we are bold to say: "Our Father…" Prayer: Lord Jesus, you were crucified for us, transfixed to the cross for our redemption, but you have transformed the instrument of death to be a tree of life and glory. Grant that we, being crucified with you, may rise with you in that kingdom where sorrow and weeping shall be no more, and your life is eternal. Amen.
4. Scripture (from the week's readings).
5. Presentation by a group member.
6. Suggested discussion questions:

   - Which of these seven words takes you closest to the heart of Christ and the Gospel, and why?
   - Does the story of the cross help you to be more forgiving and reconciling in your spectrum of relationships? How?
   - How can you apply the message of the cross: to your personal life; to your church life; to your social/political life?
   - What has this Lent course given to you, and are there elements you would like to have seen included, or omitted?